HAL•LEONARD®
GUITAR PLAY-ALONG

VOL. 129

AUDIO
ACCESS
INCLUDED

PLAYBACK+
Speed • Pitch • Balance • Loop

Cover photo courtesy of Capitol Records

ISBN 978-1-4234-9682-3

HAL•LEONARD®
7777 W. BLUEMOUND RD. P.O. BOX 13819 MILWAUKEE, WI 53213

In Australia Contact:
Hal Leonard Australia Pty. Ltd.
4 Lentara Court
Cheltenham, Victoria, 3192 Australia
Email: ausadmin@halleonard.com.au

Visit Hal Leonard Online at
www.halleonard.com

GUITAR PLAY-ALONG

AUDIO ACCESS INCLUDED

VOL. 129

CONTENTS

Hangar 18

Words and Music by Dave Mustaine

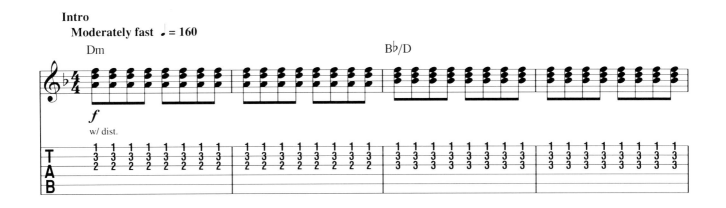

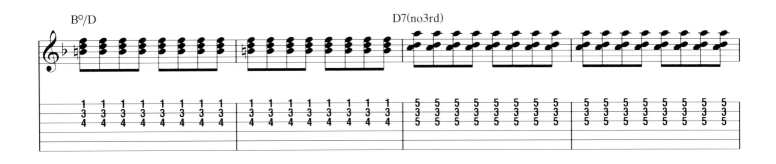

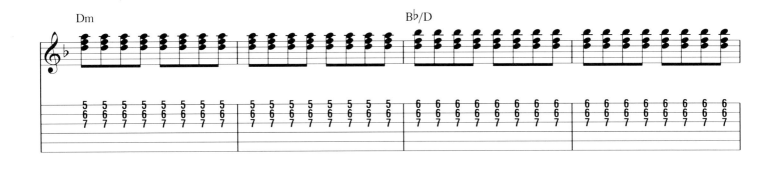

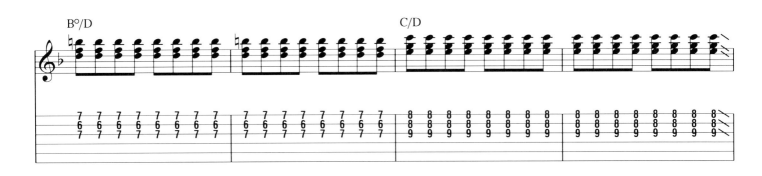

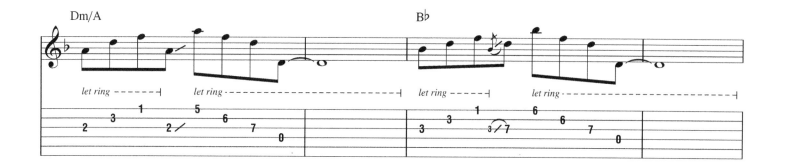

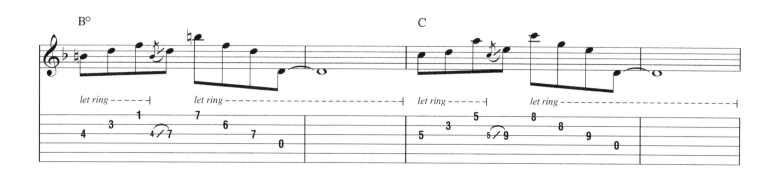

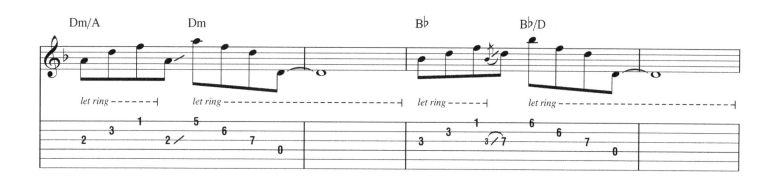

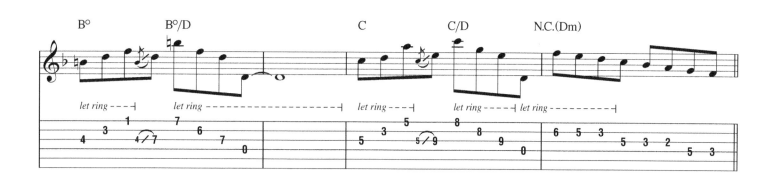

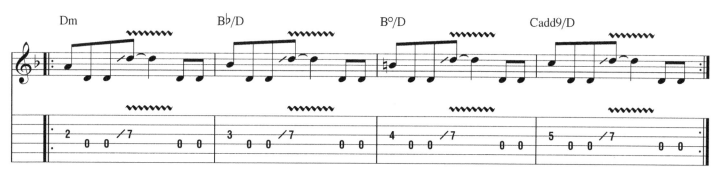

Chorus

bly I've ___ seen too much. ___ Hang - ar eight - een. ___ I

Interlude

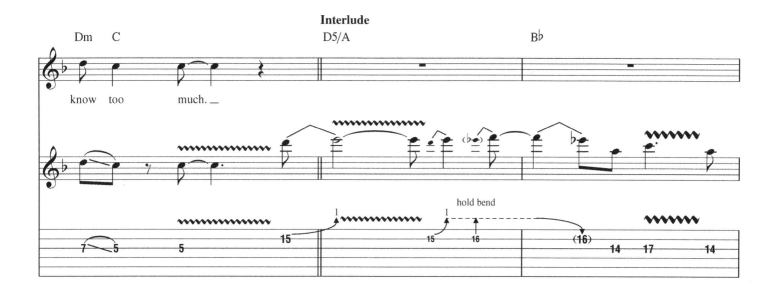

know too much. ___

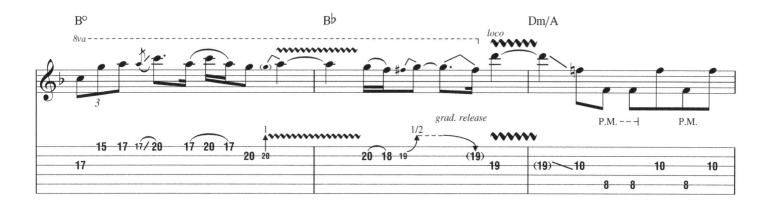

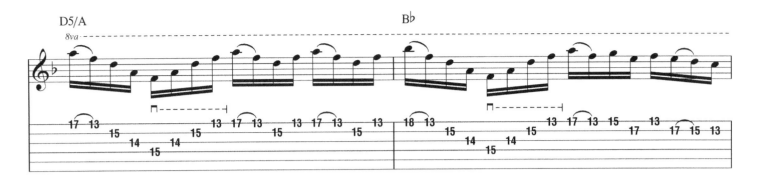

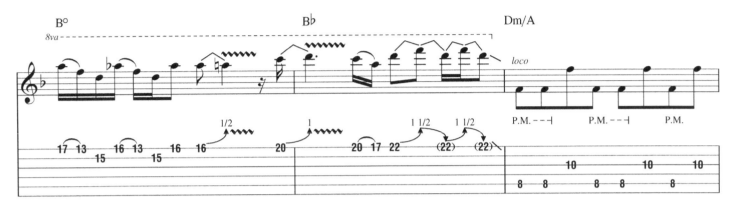

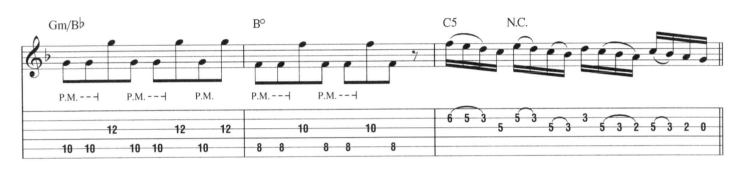

2nd time, D.S. al Coda

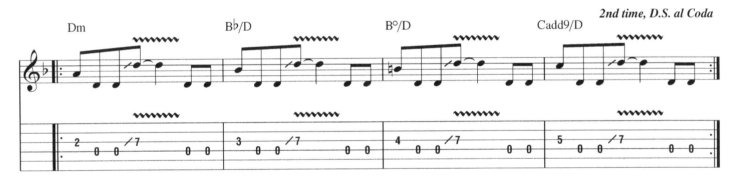

$\oplus$ Coda

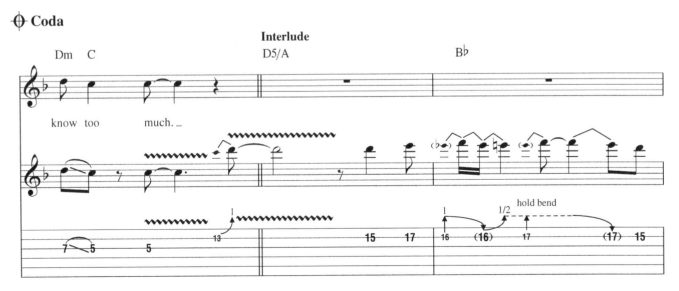

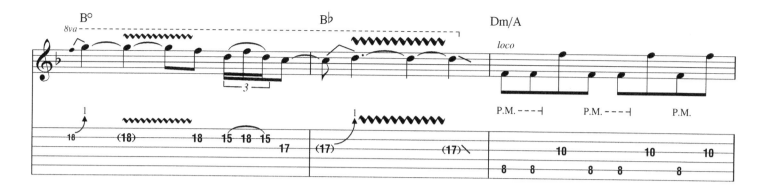

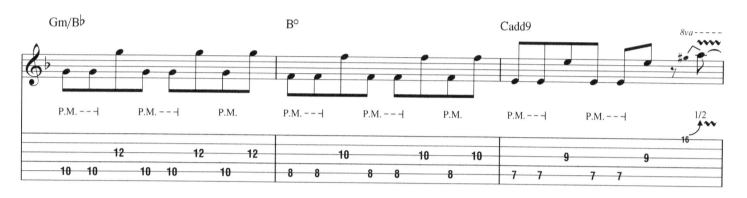

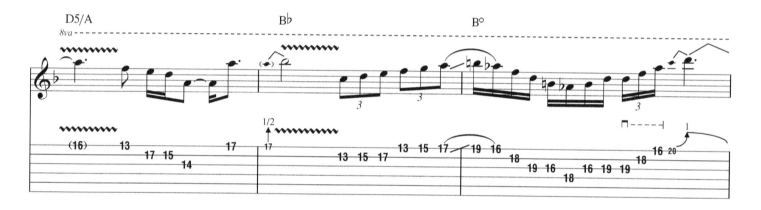

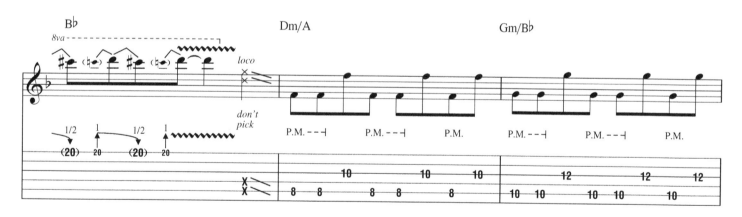

Guitar Solo
Slower ♩ = 113

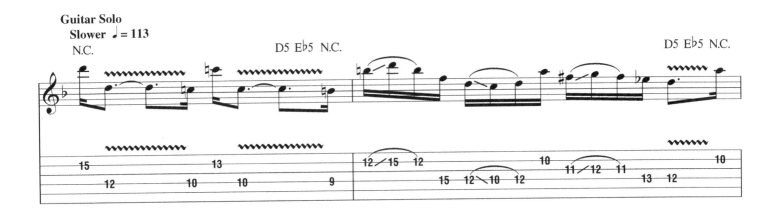

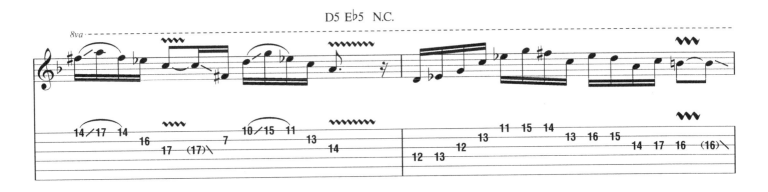

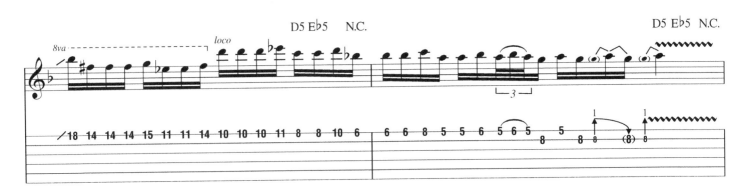

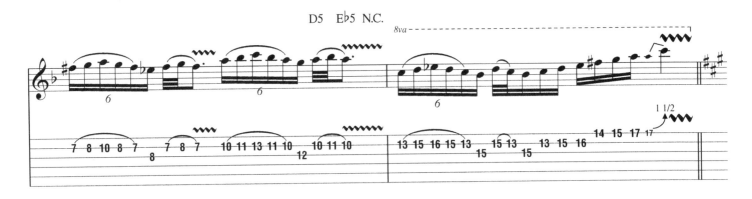

Interlude

Guitar Solo

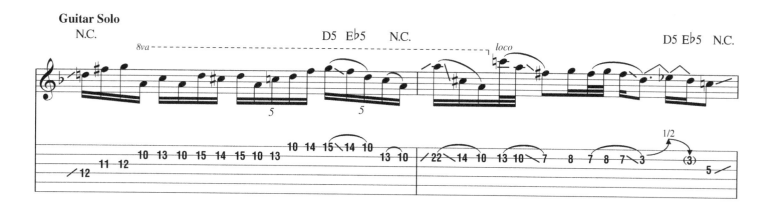

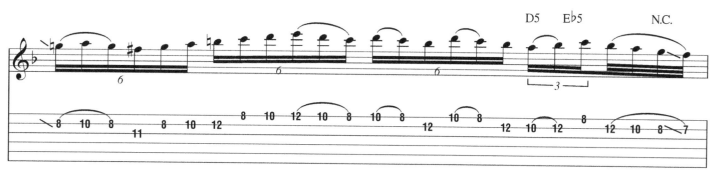

Interlude

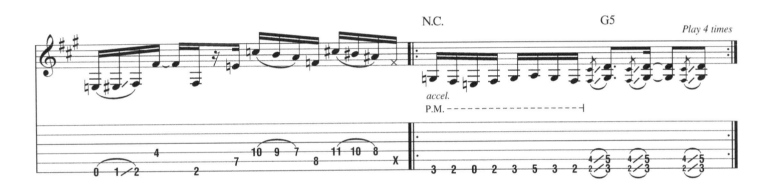

Guitar Solo
Slightly faster ♩ = 124

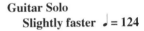

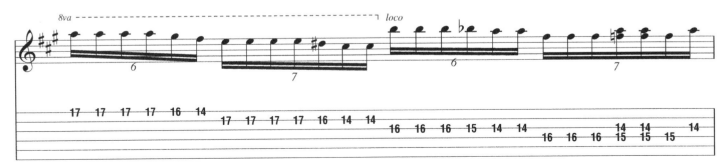

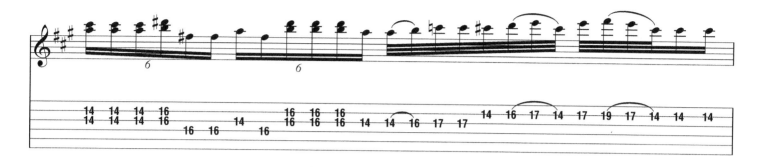

Interlude

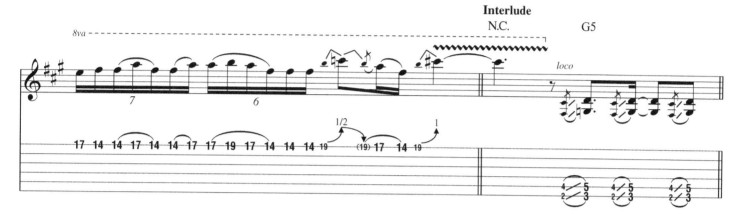

Guitar Solo

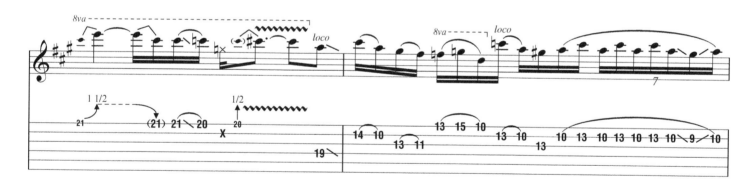

Interlude

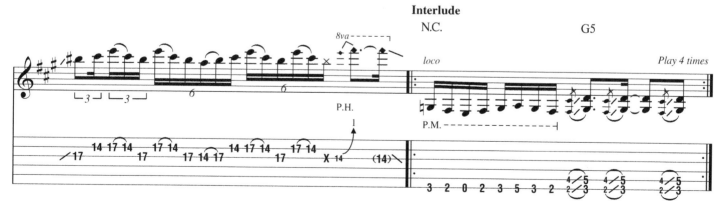

Guitar Solo

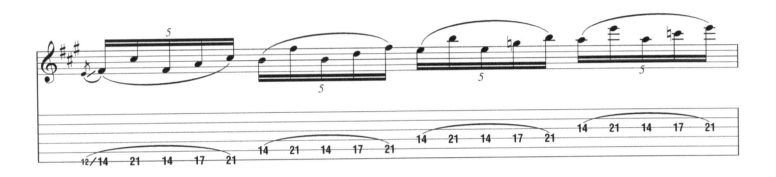

Interlude

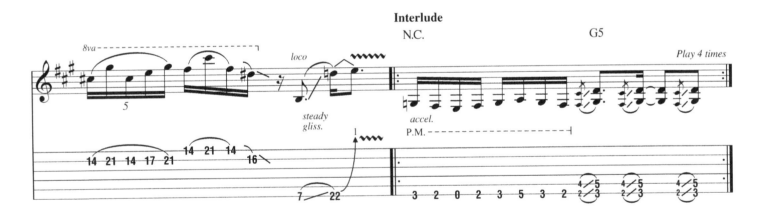

Guitar Solo
Slightly faster ♩ = 130

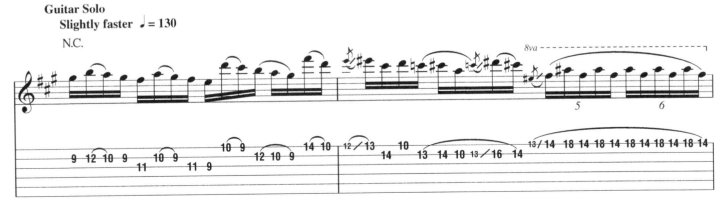

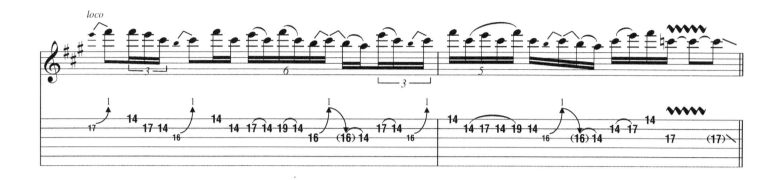

Interlude

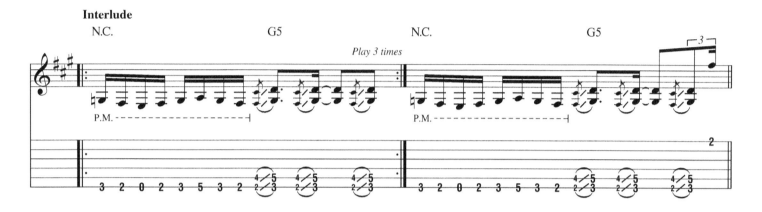

Guitar Solo

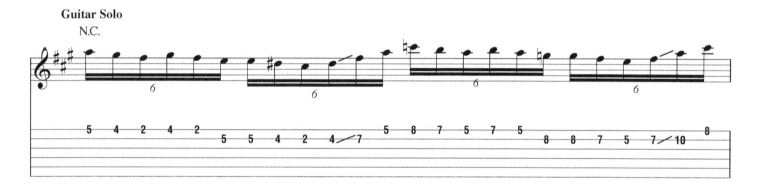

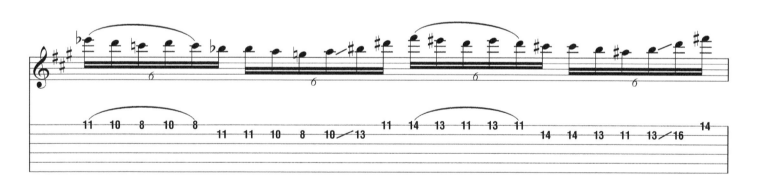

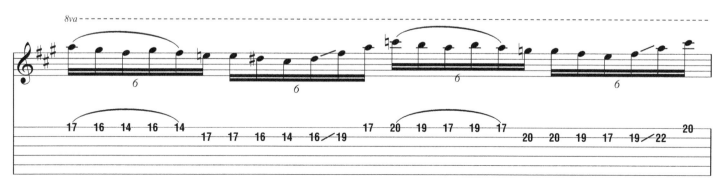

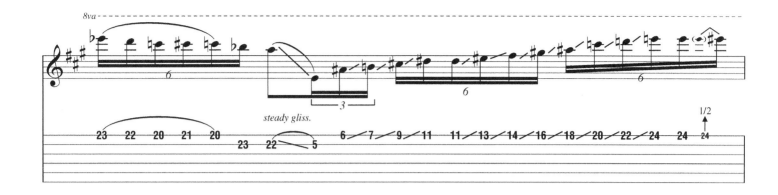

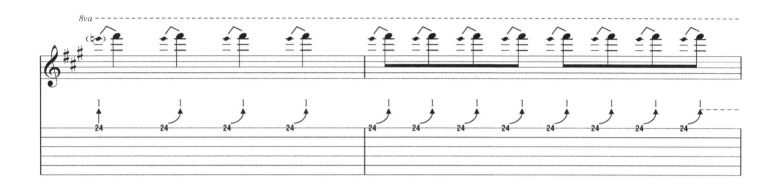

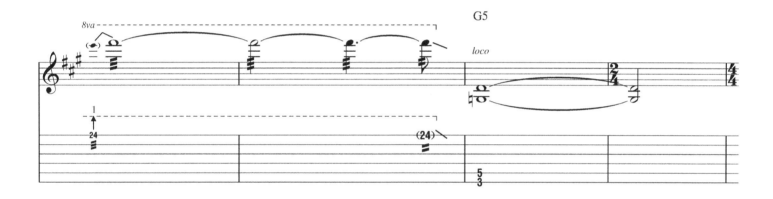

Additional Lyrics

2. Foreign life forms inventory.
   Suspended state of cryogenics.
   Selective amnesia's the story.
   Believed foretold but who'd suspect...
   The military intelligence?
   Two words combined that can't make sense.

Trust

Words and Music by Dave Mustaine and Marty Friedman

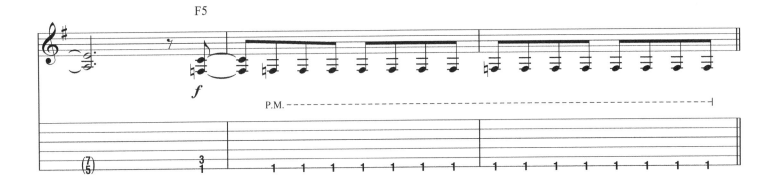

Interlude

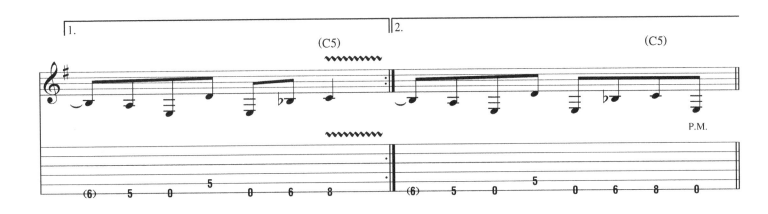

Verse

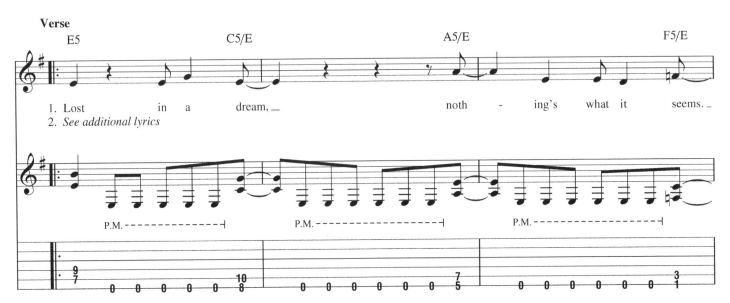

1. Lost in a dream, __ noth - ing's what it seems. __
2. *See additional lyrics*

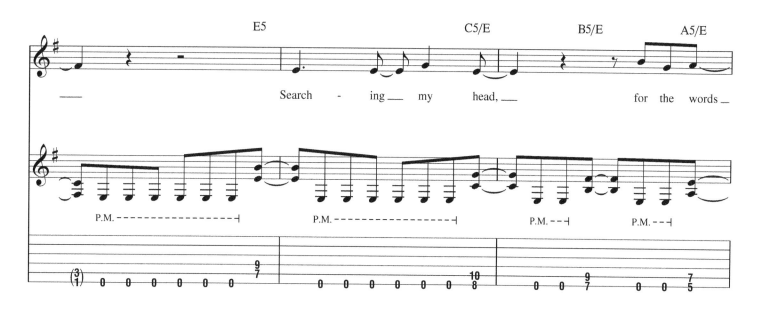

Search - ing ___ my head, ___ for the words ___

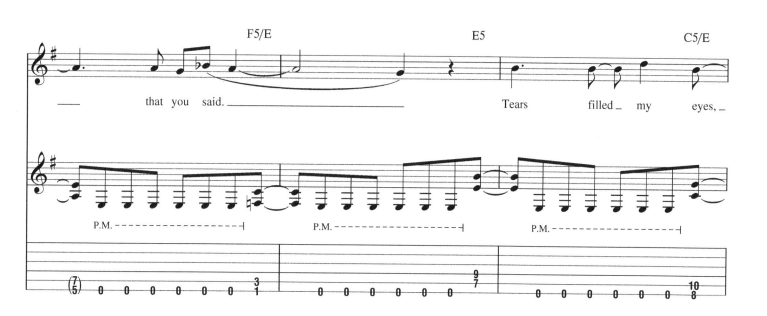

___ that you said. ___ Tears filled ___ my eyes, ___

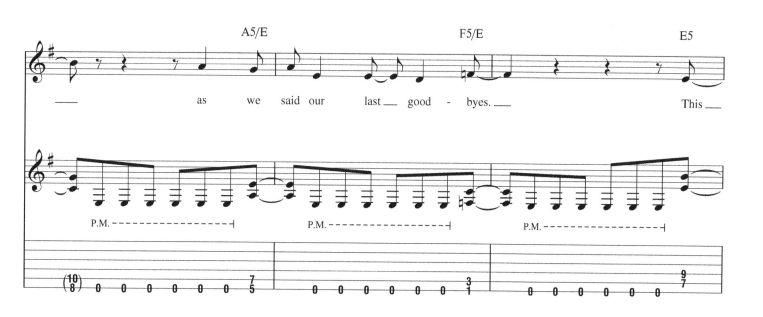

___ as we said our last ___ good - byes. ___ This ___

19

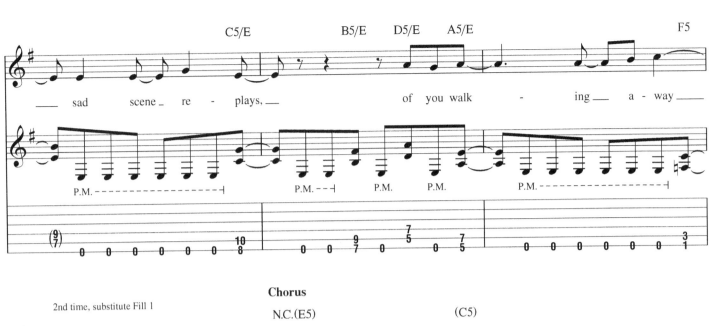

C5/E   B5/E D5/E A5/E   F5

sad scene re-plays, __ of you walk - ing __ a - way __

Chorus

2nd time, substitute Fill 1

N.C.(E5)   (C5)

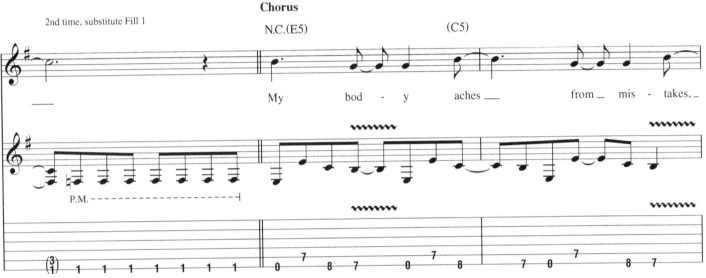

My bod - y aches __ from __ mis - takes, _

(A5)   (B♭5)   (C5) (E5)   (C5)

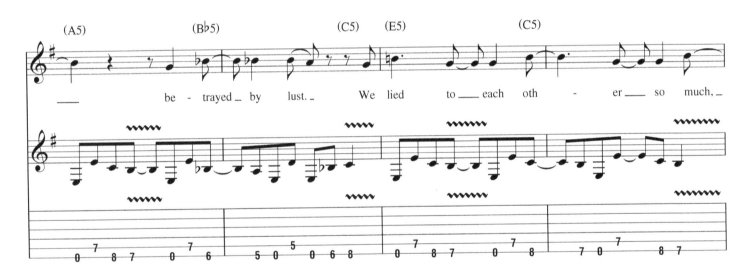

be - trayed __ by lust. _ We lied to __ each oth - er __ so much,

Fill 1

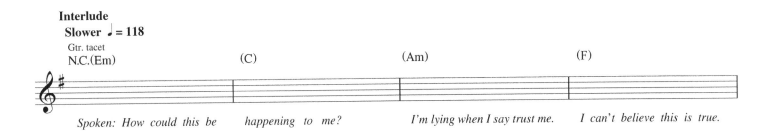

Interlude
Slower ♩ = 118

Spoken: How could this be   happening to me?   I'm lying when I say trust me.   I can't believe this is true.

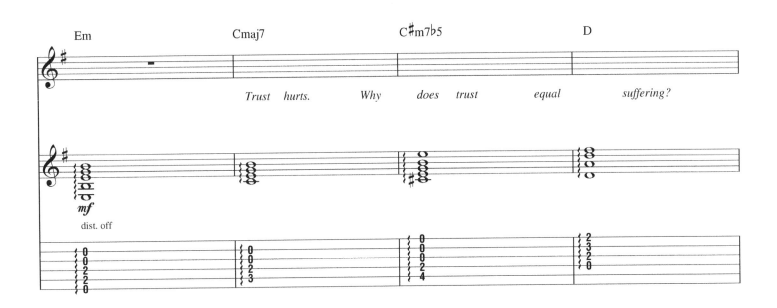

Trust   hurts.   Why   does   trust   equal   suffering?

Slightly slower ♩ = 114

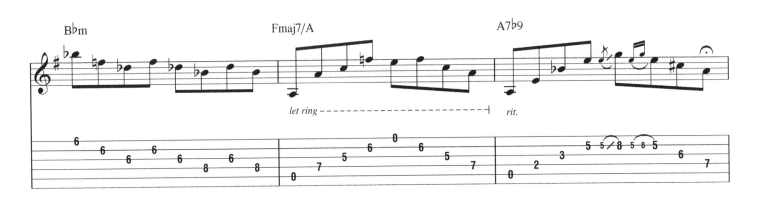

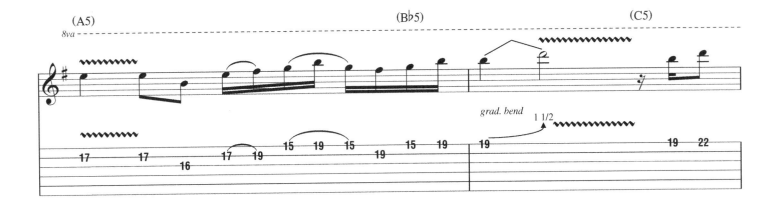

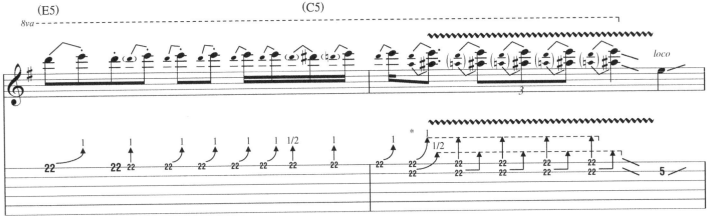

*Allow 2nd string to be caught under ring finger.

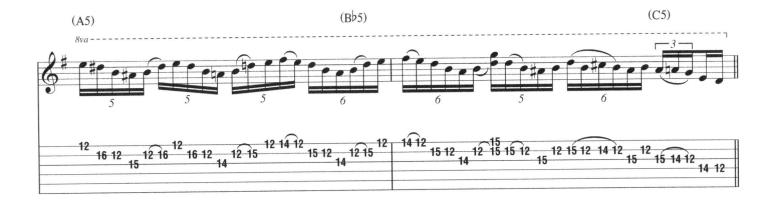

Chorus

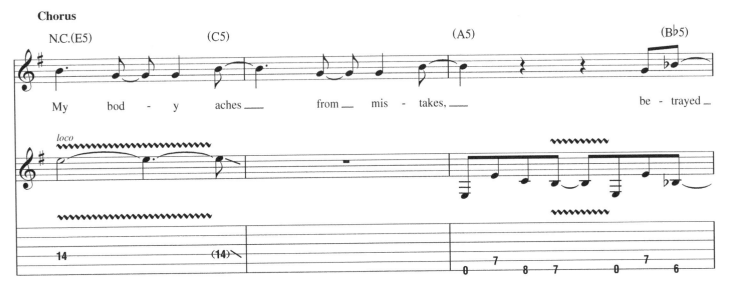

My bod - y aches _____ from _____ mis - takes, _____ be - trayed _____

*Vol. knob swell.

Additional Lyrics

2. Time and again,
She repeats, "Let's be friends."
I smile and say yes.
Another truth bends, I must confess.
I try to let go,
But I know we'll never end 'til we're dust.
We lied to each other again.
(I wish I could trust.)
But I wish I could trust.

Head Crusher

Words and Music by Dave Mustaine and Shawn Drover

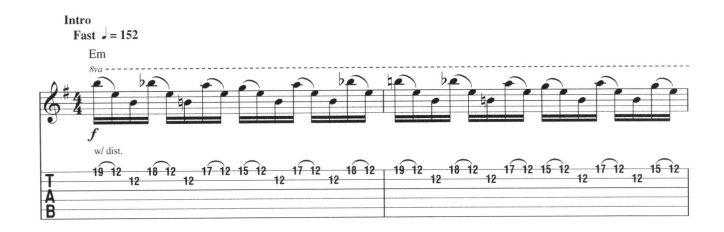

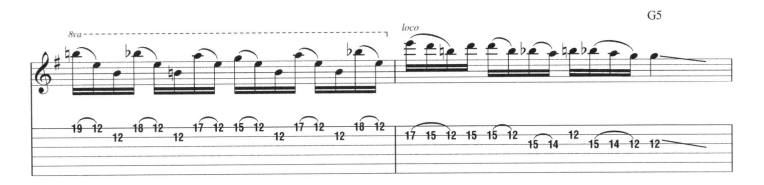

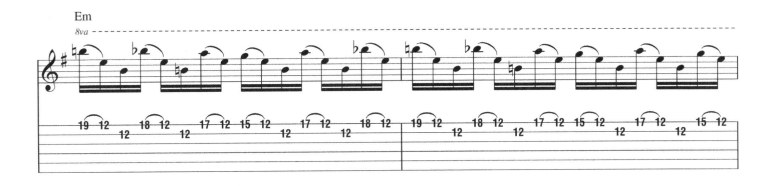

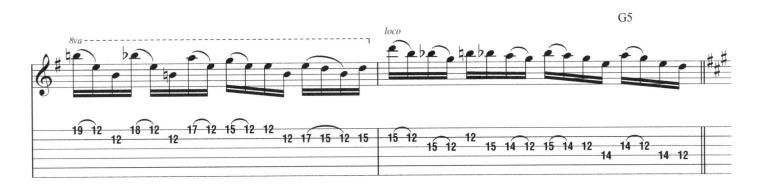

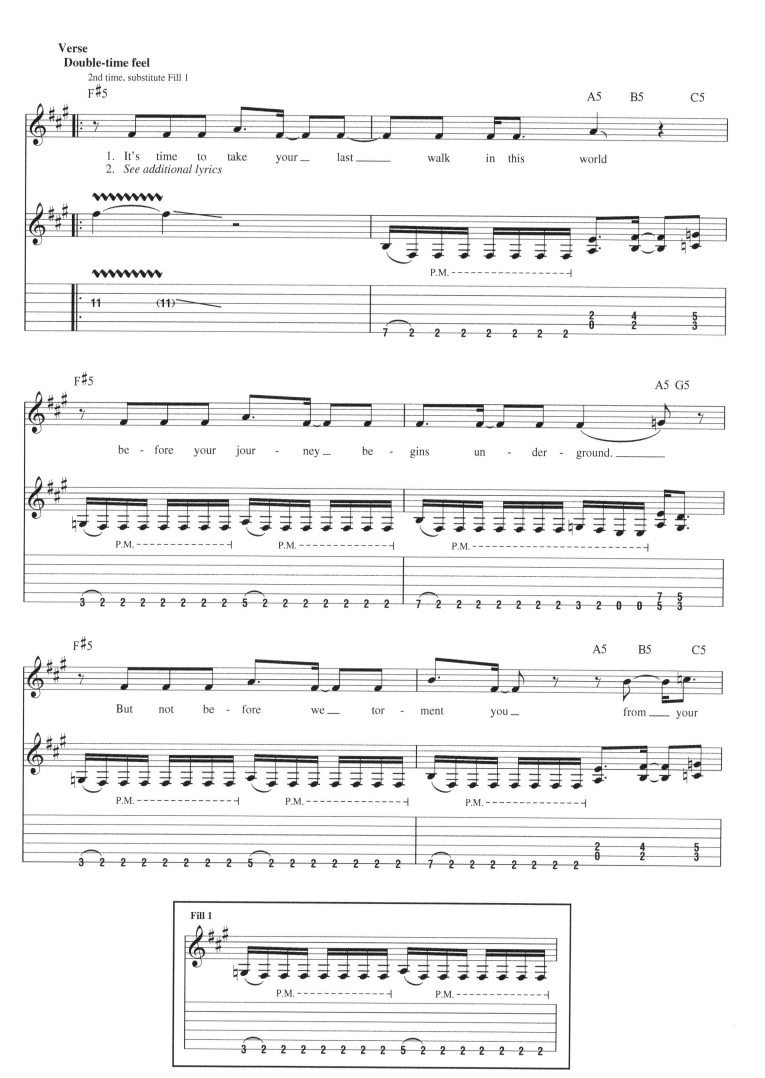

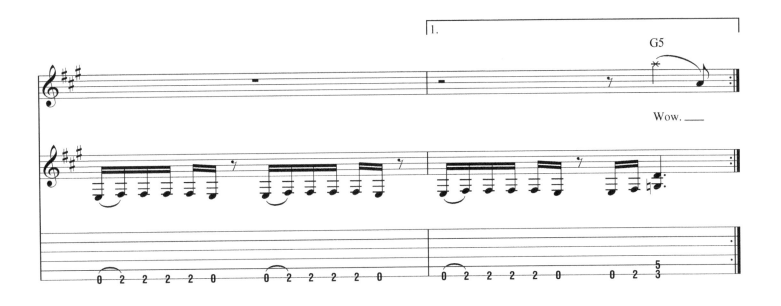

Wow. ___

Bridge

Spoken: On your knees, pris-'ner, and take your po - si - tion.

let ring

P.M.

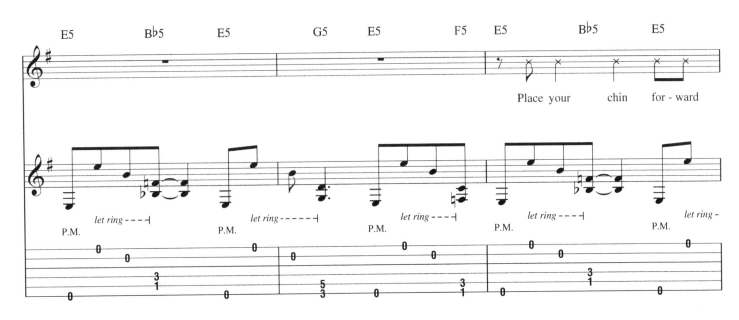

Place your chin for - ward

let ring

P.M.

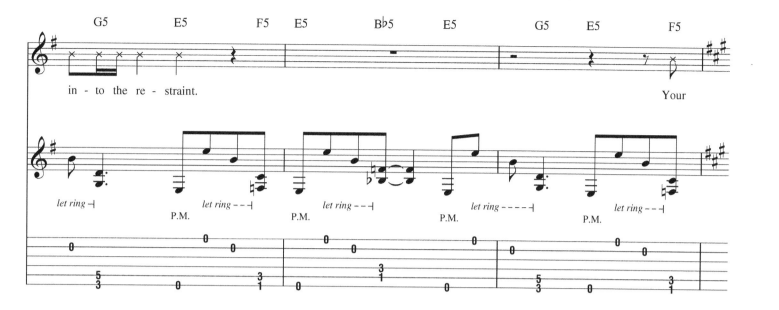

Bridge

Twist - ing,_____ turn - ing the gi - ant screw,_

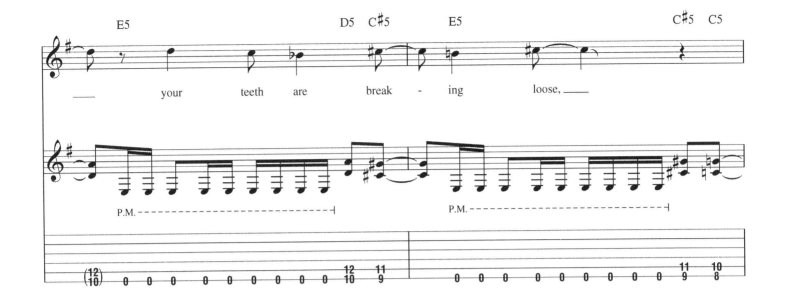

Outro-Guitar Solo

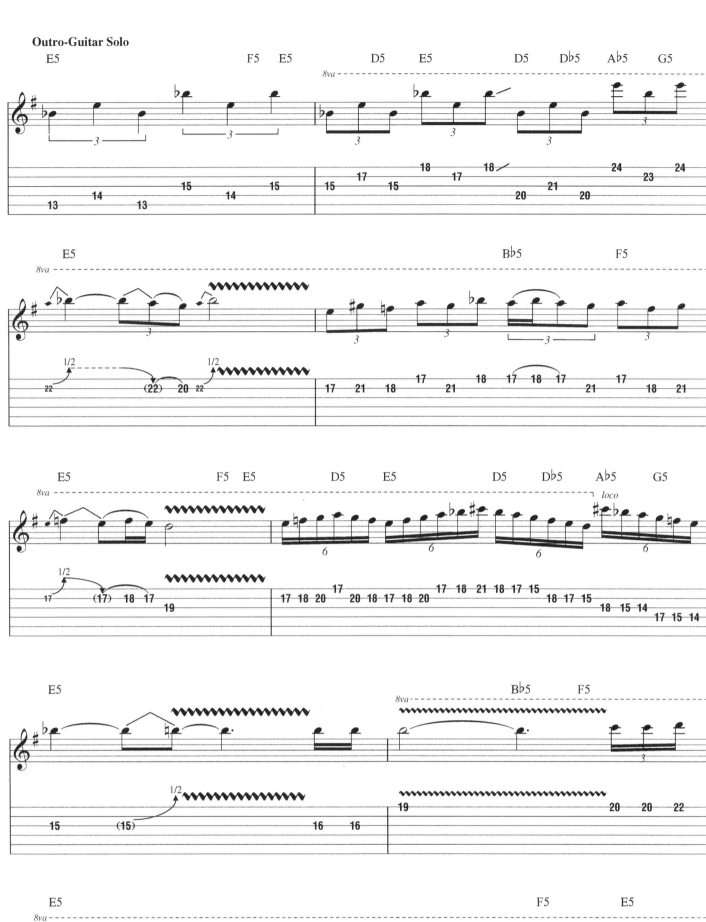

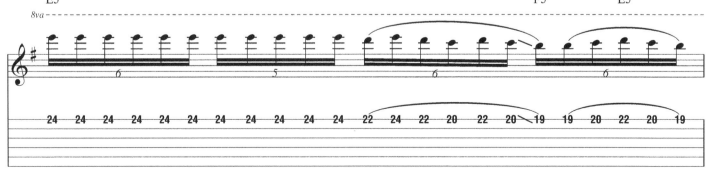

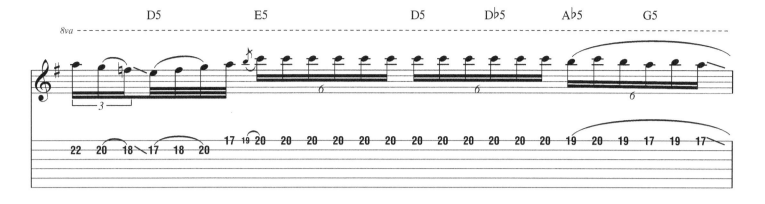

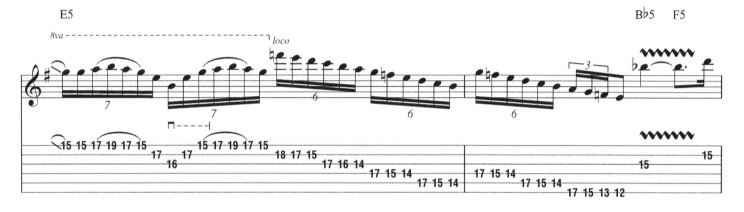

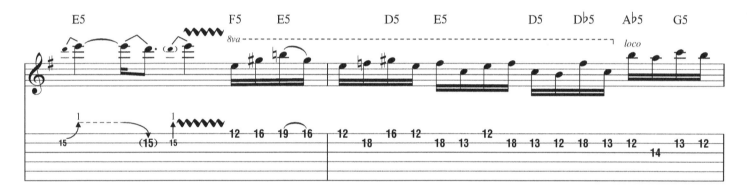

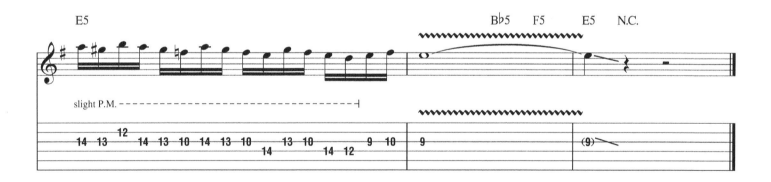

Additional Lyrics

2. The horrific torture device
   For those who fail interrogation.
   The most painful technique ever known.
   People thirst for the worst:
   The skull's disintegration.
   Beaten, broken, in bloody rags.
   Adding insult to injury.
   He recants, but it's much too late.

Holy Wars... The Punishment Due

Words and Music by Dave Mustaine

Intro
Moderately fast ♩ = 164

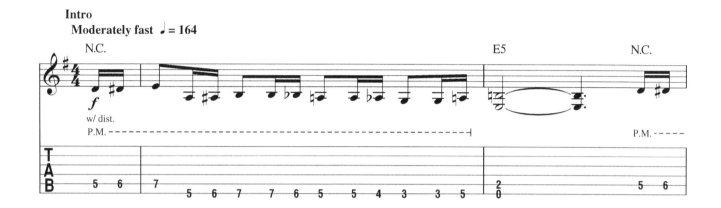

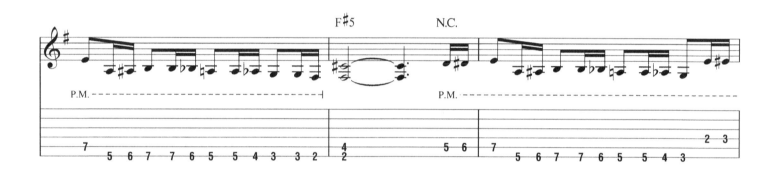

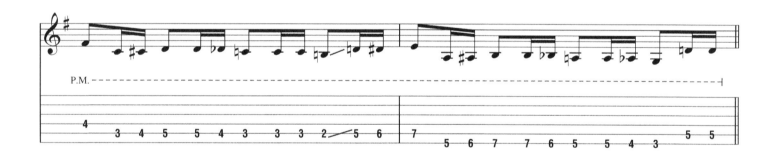

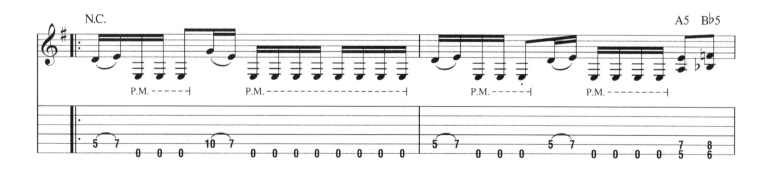

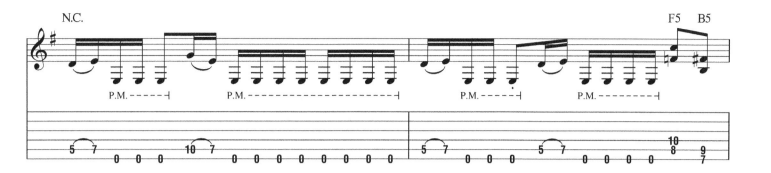

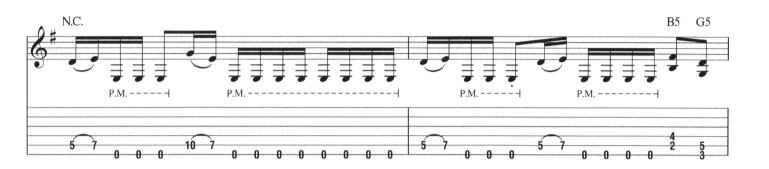

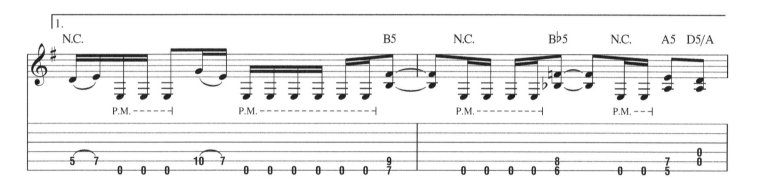

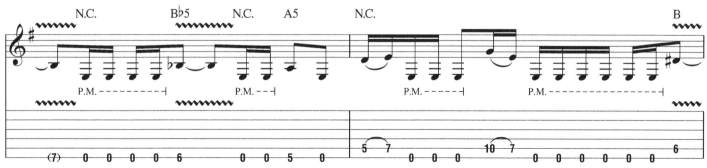

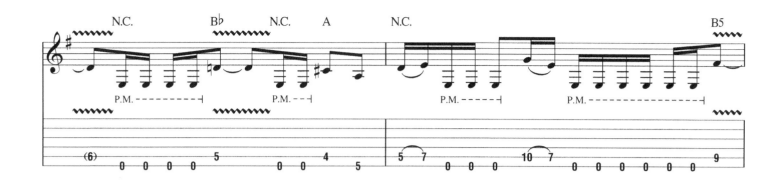

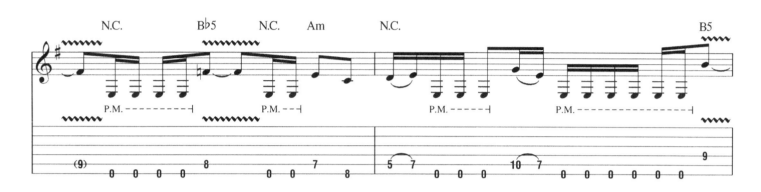

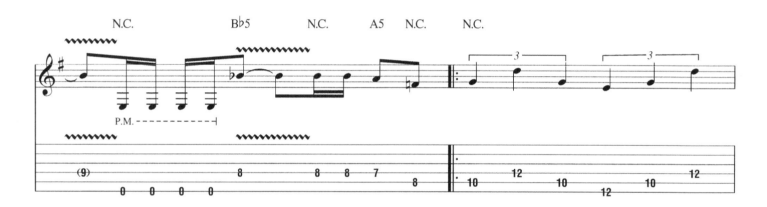

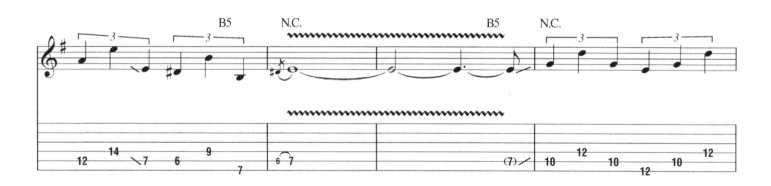

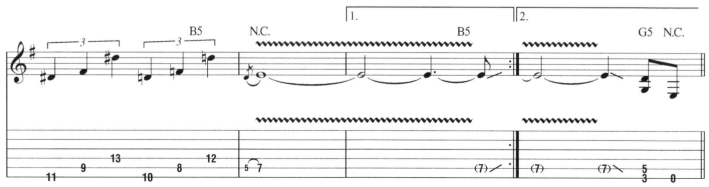

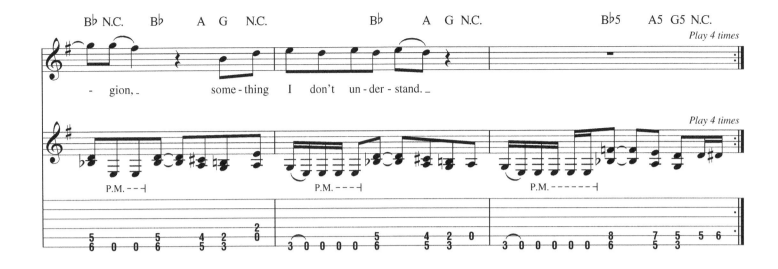

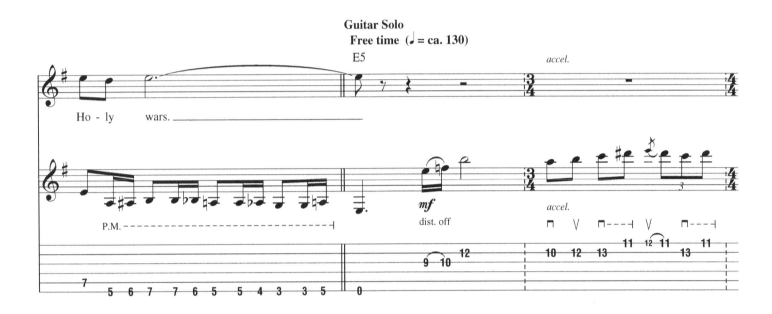

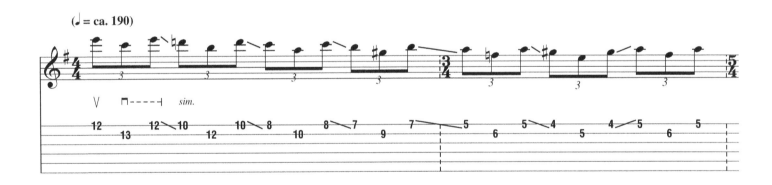

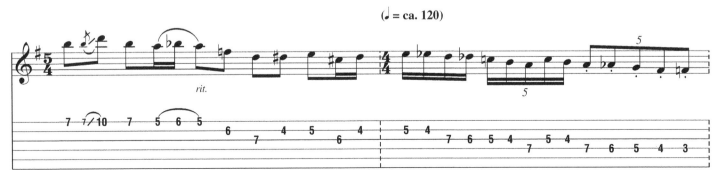

Guitar Solo

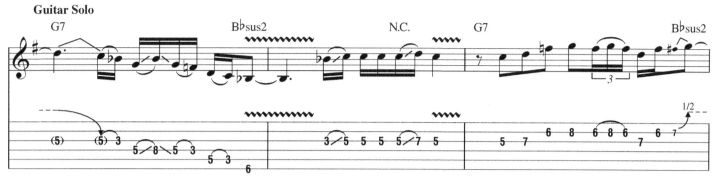

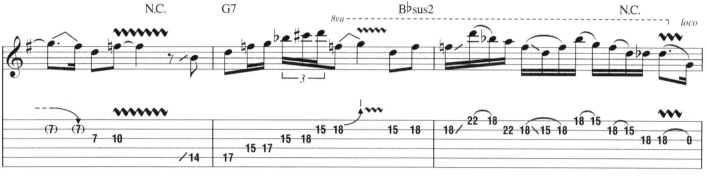

Interlude
Faster ♩ = 180

End half-time feel

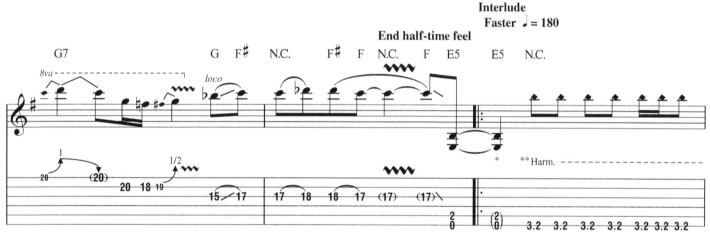

*Strike chord on repeat.
**Mute string near 3rd fret, sounding slight harmonic.

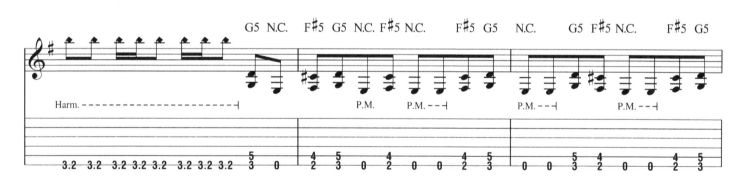

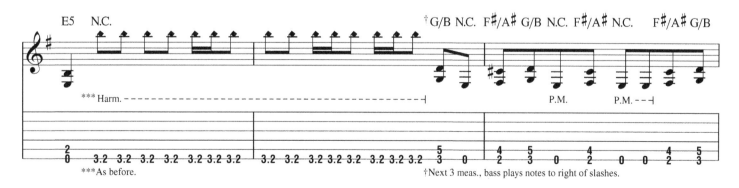

***As before.

†Next 3 meas., bass plays notes to right of slashes.

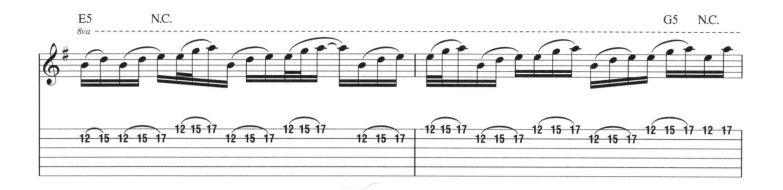

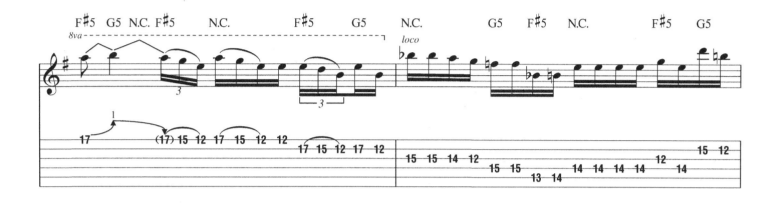

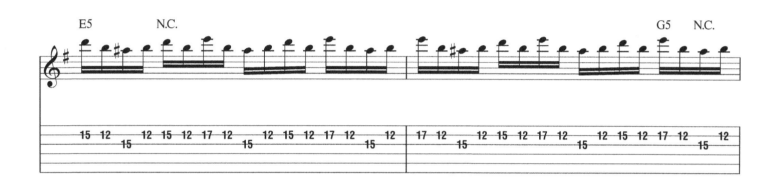

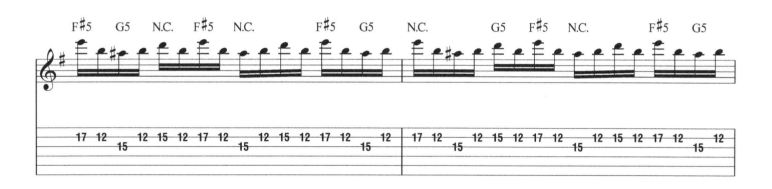

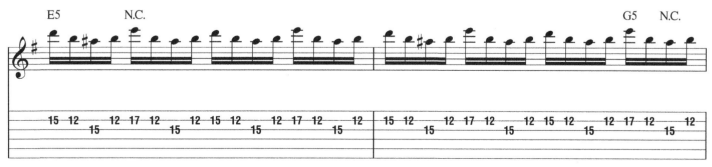

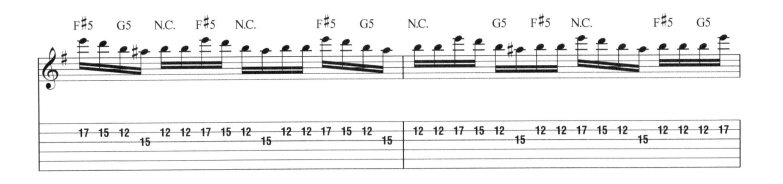

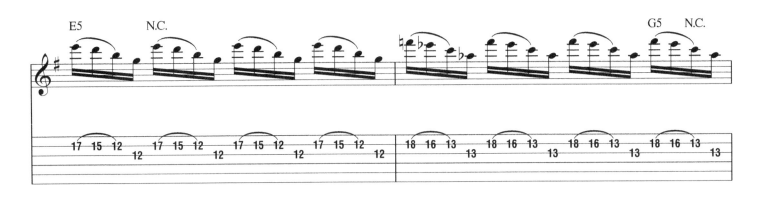

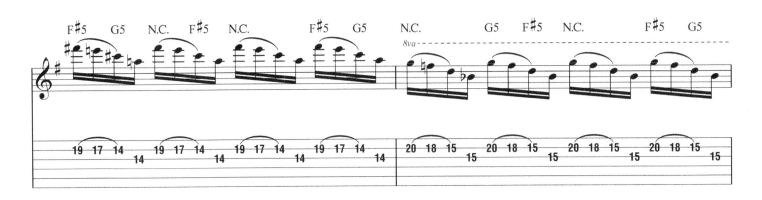

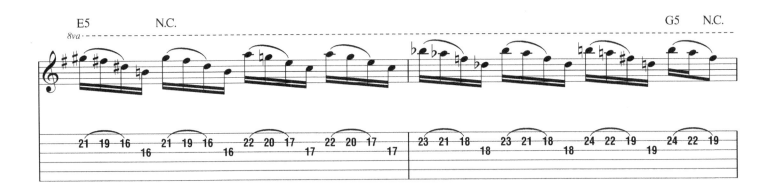

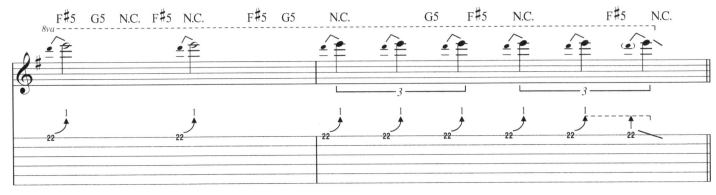

Additional Lyrics

2. Fools like me, who cross the sea,
   And come to foreign lands,
   Ask the sheep, for their beliefs,
   Do you kill on God's command?

3. A country that's divided
   Surely will not stand.
   My past erased, no more disgrace.
   No foolish naive stand.

4. The end is near, it's crystal clear,
   Part of the master plan.
   Don't look now to Israel.
   It might be your homeland.
   Holy wars.

6. They killed my wife and my baby
   With hopes to enslave me.
   First mistake... last mistake!
   Paid by the alliance, to slay all the giants.
   Next mistake... no more mistakes!

Peace Sells

Words and Music by Dave Mustaine

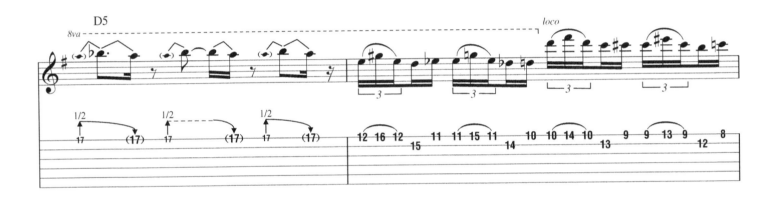

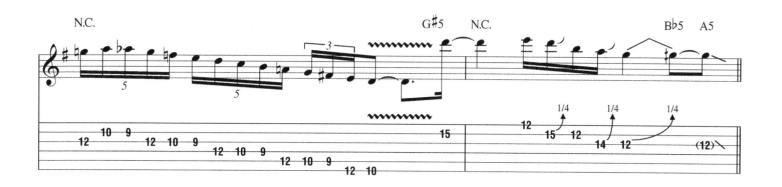

Verse

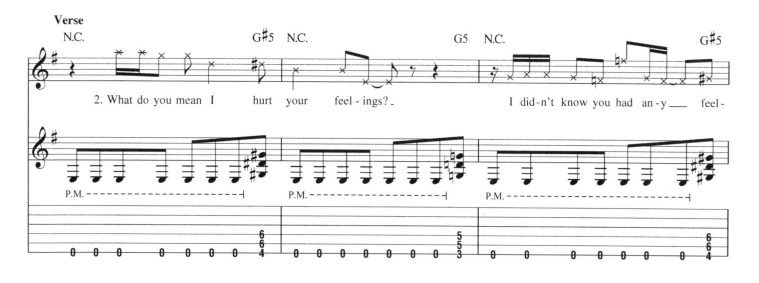

2. What do you mean I hurt your feel-ings? _ I did-n't know you had an-y _ feel-

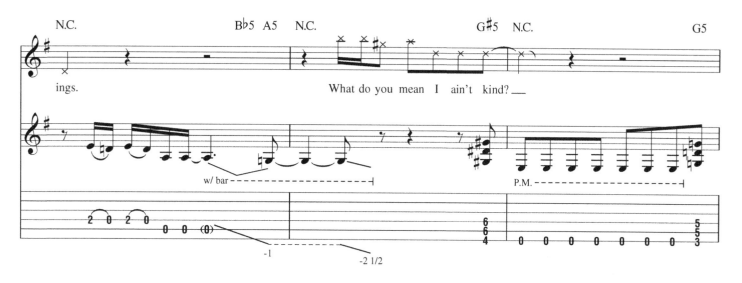

ings. What do you mean I ain't kind? _

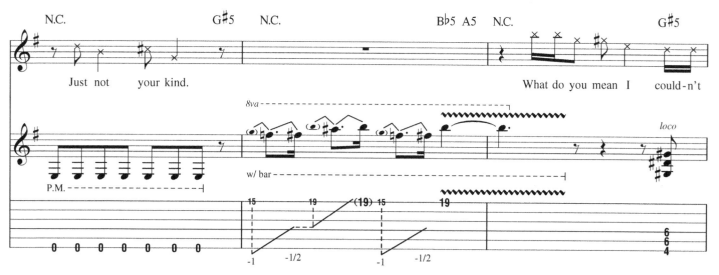

Just not your kind. What do you mean I could-n't

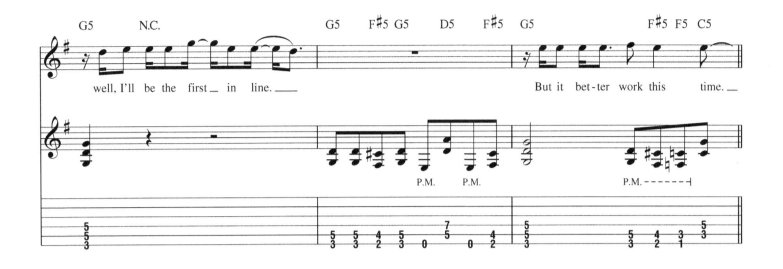

well, I'll be the first __ in line. ___   But it bet-ter work this   time. __

Interlude

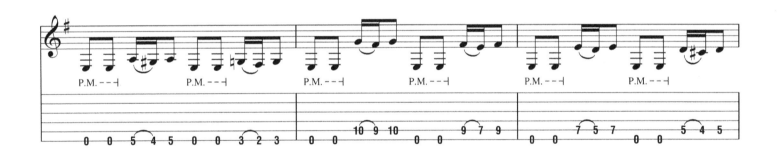

Guitar Break

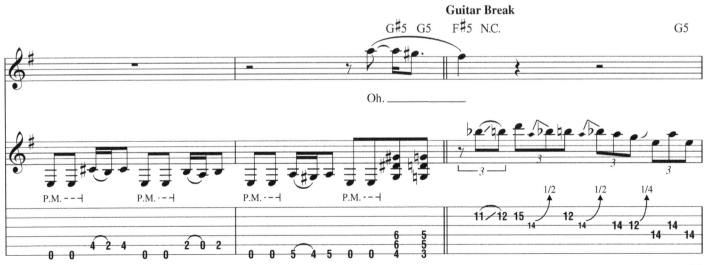

Oh. ___

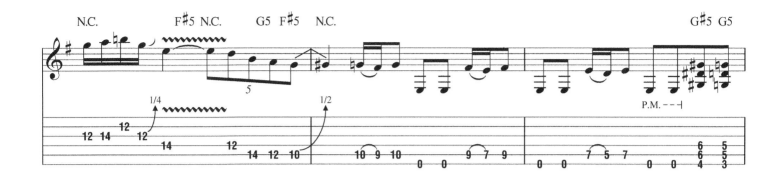

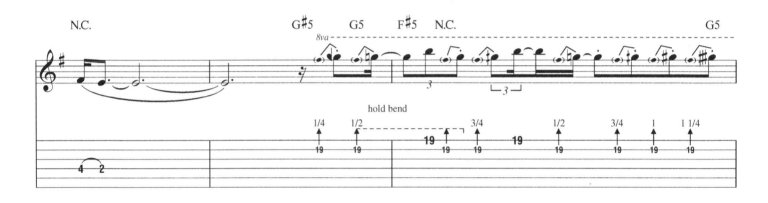

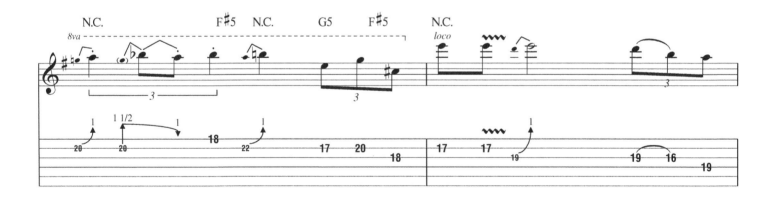

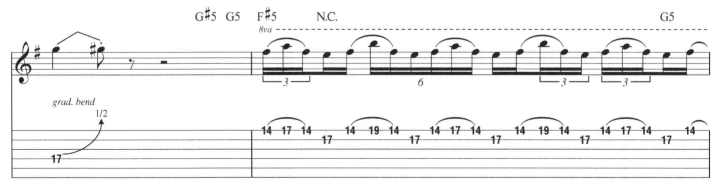

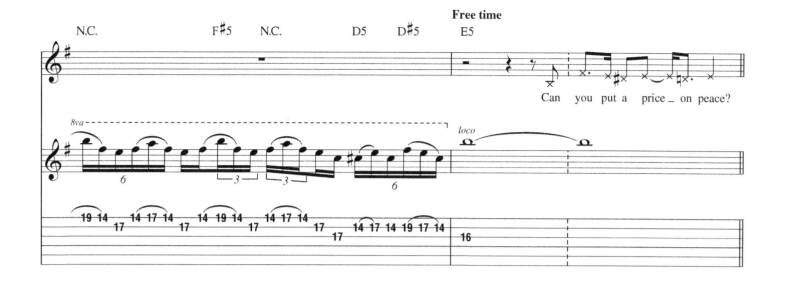

Can you put a price __ on peace?

Interlude
Faster ♩ = 162

Bridge

Peace,   peace   sells. _____

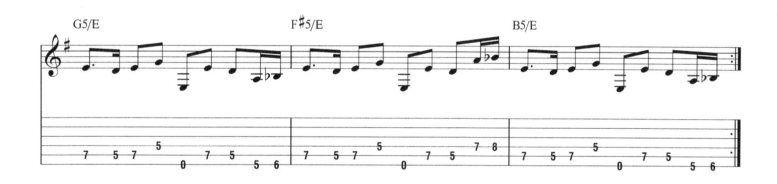

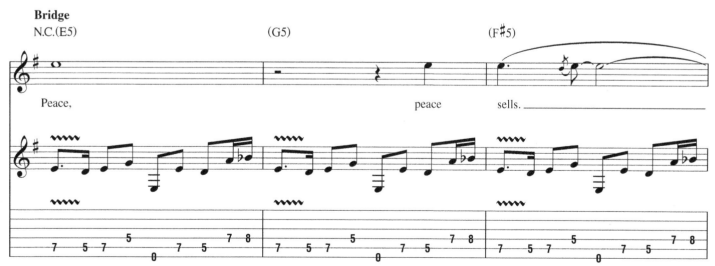

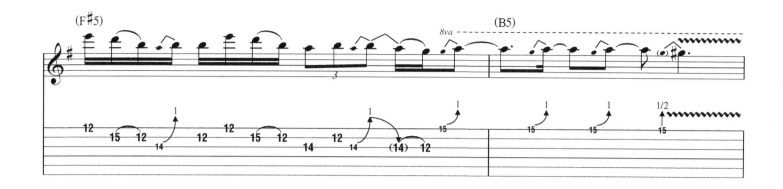

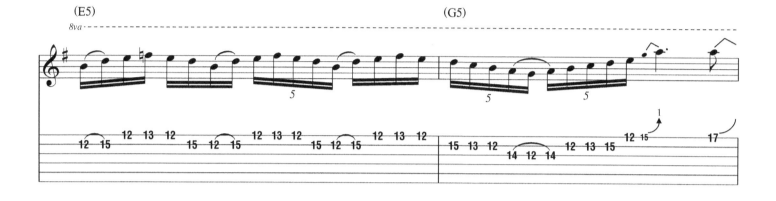

Bridge

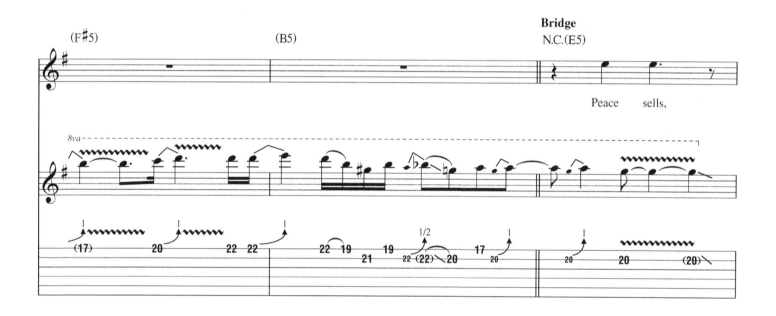

Peace sells,

but who's buy-ing?   Peace sells,   but who's buy-ing?

*Tap & bend w/ index finger while holding pick between thumb & middle finger, then pick
while holding tapped note and pull off to 15th fret. Assist bends w/ fret hand till end.

Sweating Bullets

Words and Music by Dave Mustaine

Intro
Moderately slow ♩ = 82

Verse
Double-time ♩ = 164

1. *Hello, me...*   *Meet the real me,*   *and my misfit's*   *way of life.*
2., 3. *See additional lyrics*

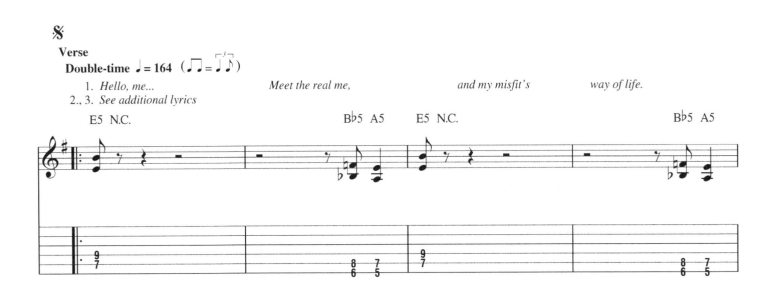

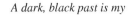

A dark, black past is my   most valued possession.

Hindsight is always twenty-twenty,   but looking back, it's still a bit fuzzy.

Speak of mutually assured destruction?   Nice story...   Tell it to Reader's Digest.

Chorus

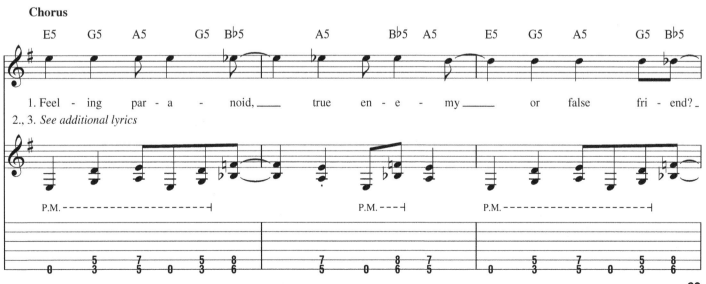

1. Feel - ing par - a - noid, ____ true en - e - my ____ or false fri - end? ____
2., 3. *See additional lyrics*

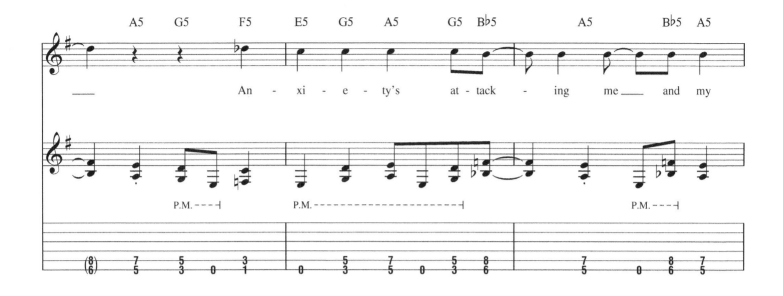

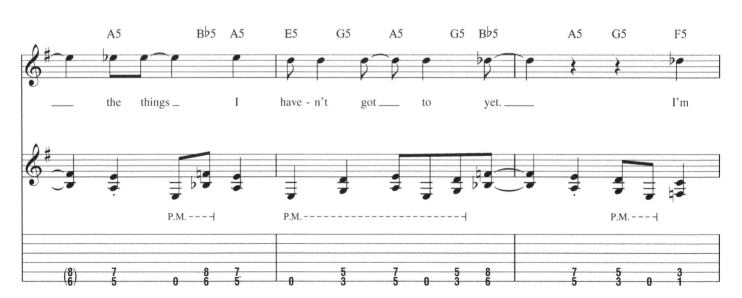

chomp - ing at the bit, ____ and ____ my palms are get - ting wet, ____

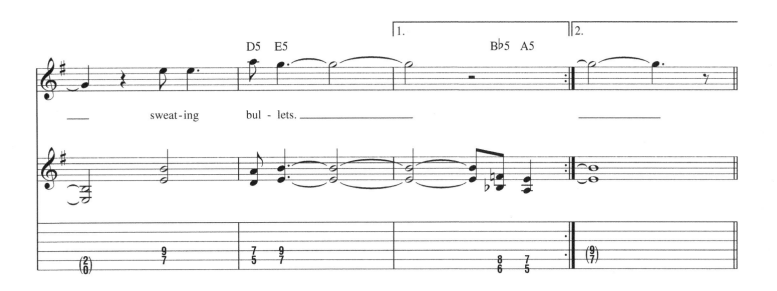

sweat - ing bul - lets. ____

Interlude

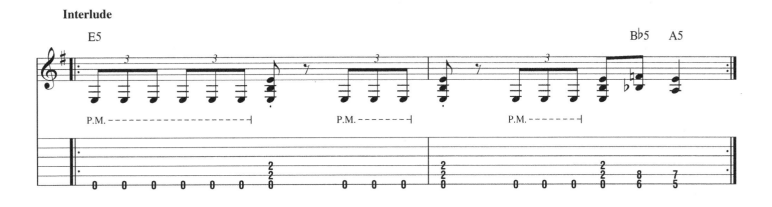

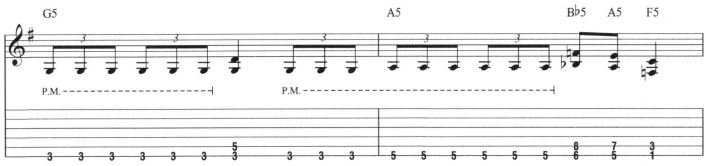

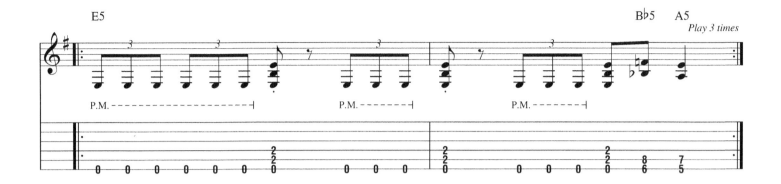

Guitar Solo

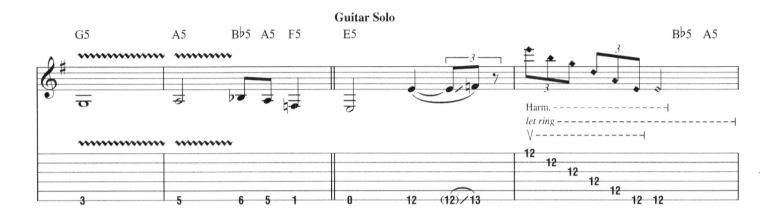

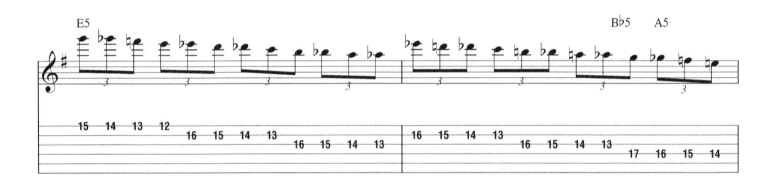

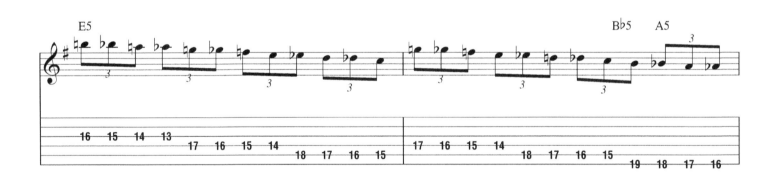

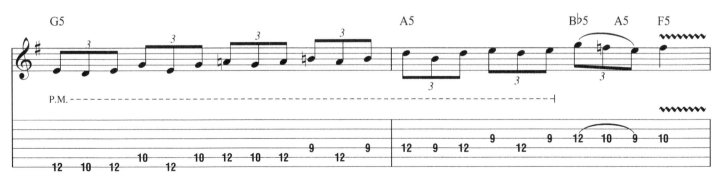

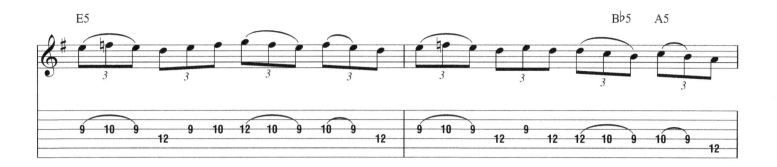

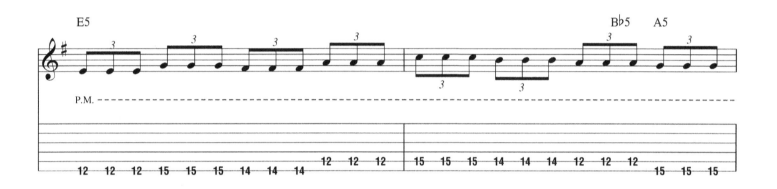

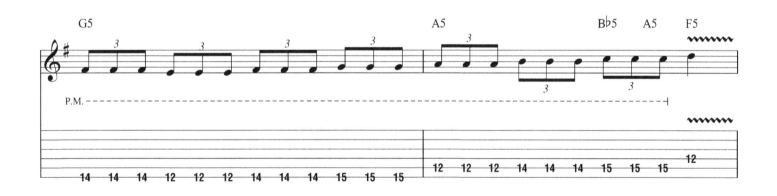

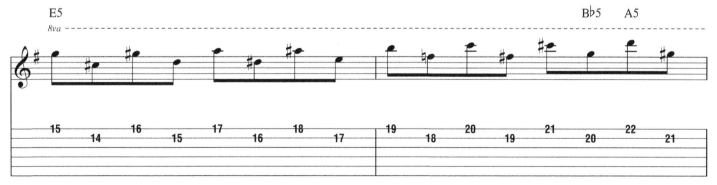

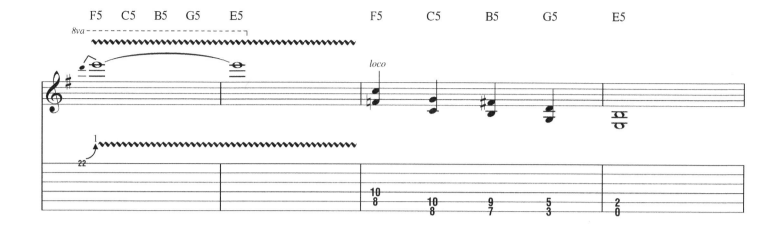

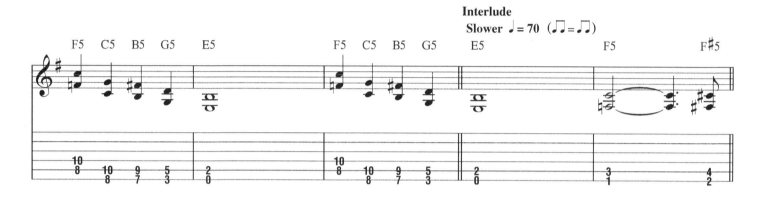

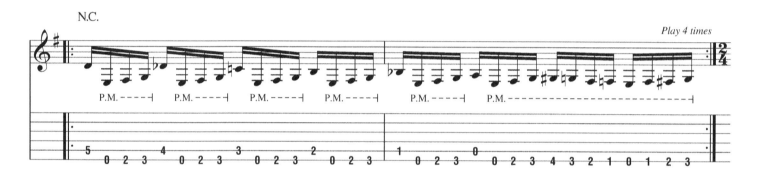

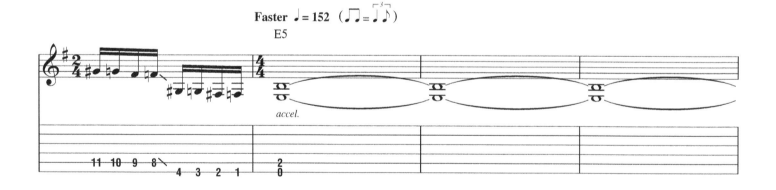

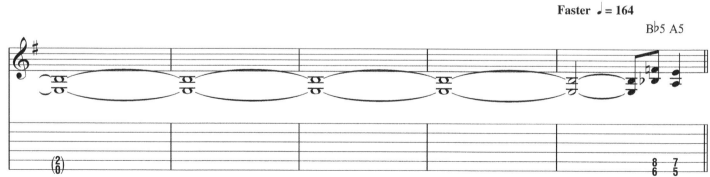

74

⊕ Coda

Outro

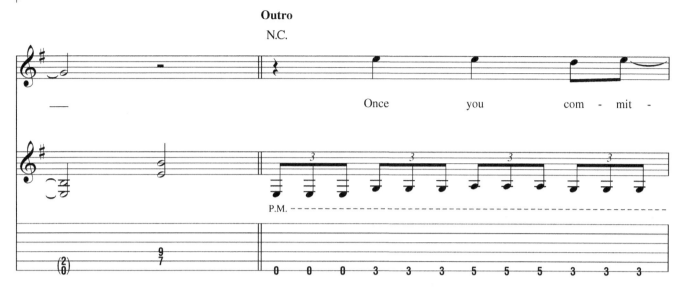

Once you com - mit -

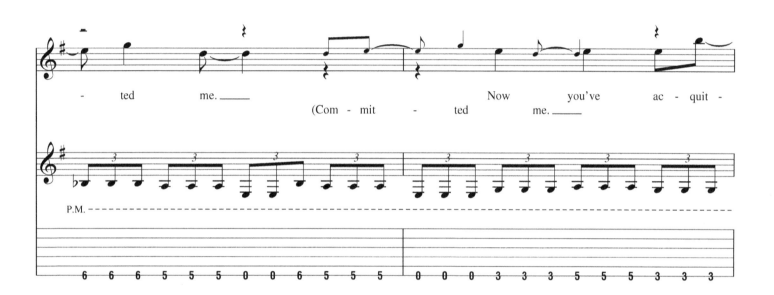

- ted me.___ Now you've ac - quit -
(Com - mit - ted me.___

- ted me.___ Claim - ing va - lid -
Ac - quit - ted me.___

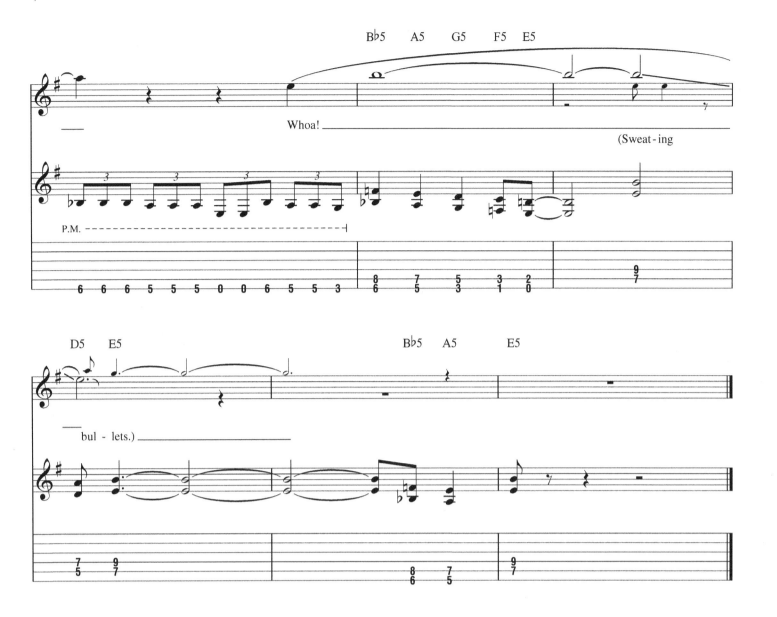

Additional Lyrics

2. Hello me... It's me again.
You can subdue, but never tame me.
It gives me a migraine headache
Thinking down to your level.
Yea, just keep on thinking it's my fault.
And stay an inch or two outta kicking distance.
Mankind has got to know
His limitations.

Chorus 2. Feeling claustrophobic, like the walls are closing in.
Blood stains on my hands and I don't know where I've been.
I'm in trouble for the things I haven't got to yet.
I'm sharpening the axe and my palms are getting wet,
Sweating bullets.

3. Well me... it's nice talking to myself,
A credit to dementia.
Some day you too will know my pain,
And smile its blacktooth grin.
If the war inside my head
Won't take a day off I'll be dead.
My icy fingers claw your back,
Here I come again.

Chorus 3. Feeling paranoid, true enemy or false friend?
Anxiety's attacking me and my air is getting thin.
Feeling claustrophobic, like the walls are closing in.
Blood stains on my hands and I don't know where I've been.

Symphony of Destruction

Words and Music by Dave Mustaine

1. You take a mortal man
3. *See additional lyrics*

and put him in control.

Fill 1

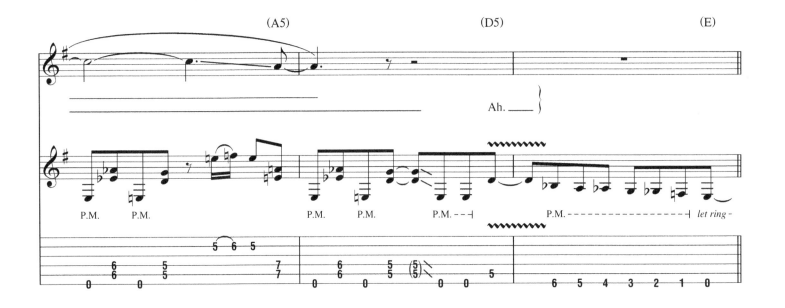

Chorus

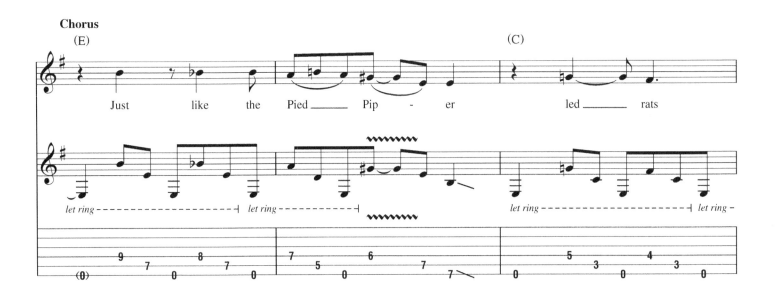

Just like the Pied ___ Pip - er led ___ rats

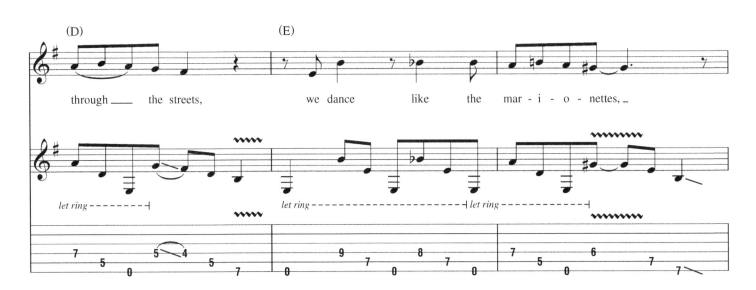

through ___ the streets, we dance like the mar - i - o - nettes, _

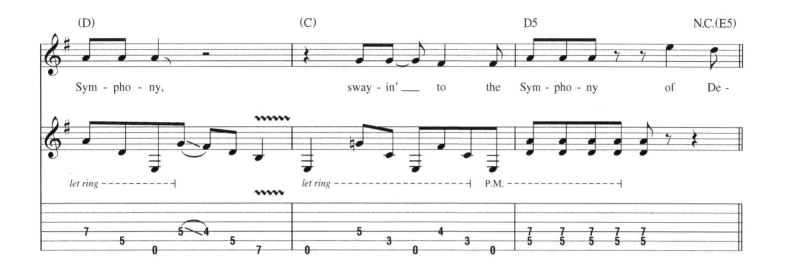

Sym - pho - ny, sway - in'___ to the Sym - pho - ny of De-

let ring P.M.

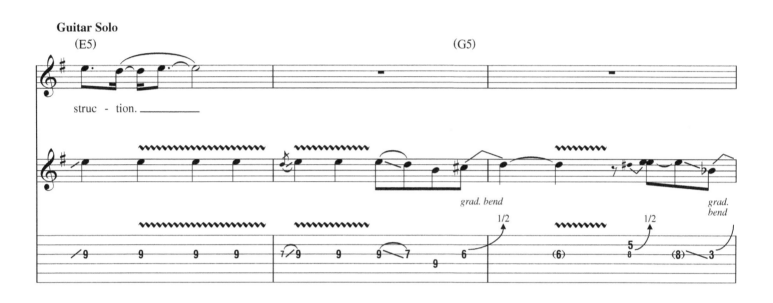

Guitar Solo

struc - tion.___

grad. bend *grad. bend*

P.M. *grad. bend* *grad. bend*

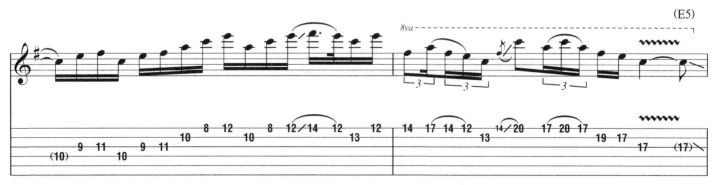

8va

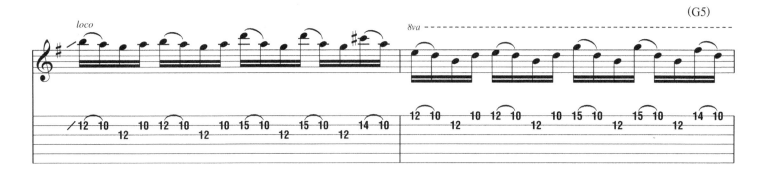

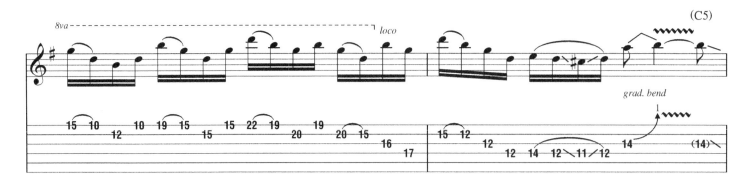

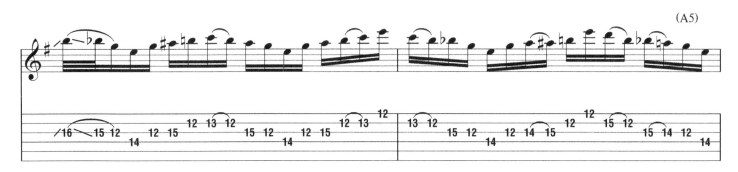

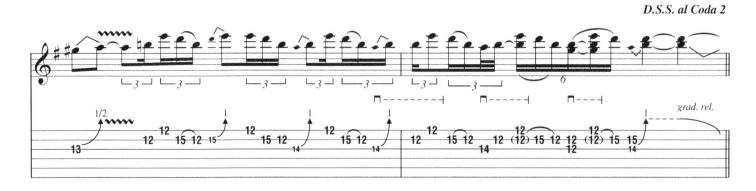

✦ Coda 2

Sym-pho-ny...   Just   like   the   Pied ____ Pip - er

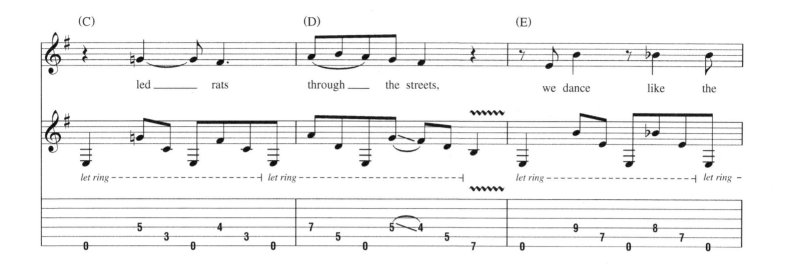

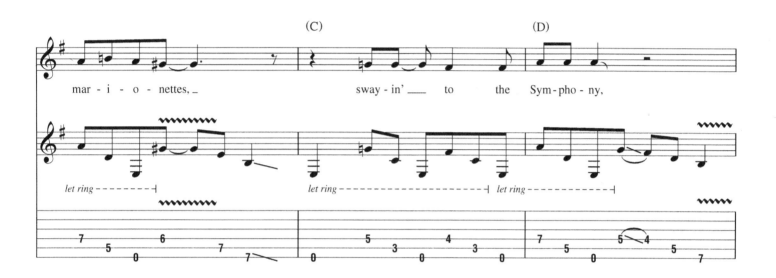

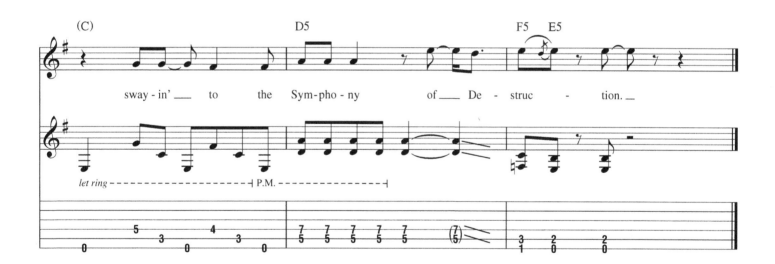

Additional Lyrics

3. The earth starts to rumble.
   World powers fall.
   A, warring for the heavens,
   A peaceful man stands tall, a, tall, a, tall.

Train of Consequences

Words and Music by Dave Mustaine, Dave Ellefson, Nick Menza and Martin Friedman

Tune down 1/2 step:
(low to high) E♭-A♭-D♭-G♭-B♭-E♭

Intro
Moderate Rock ♩ = 114

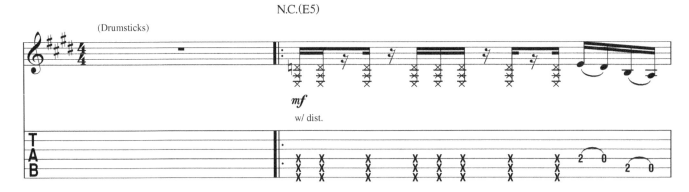

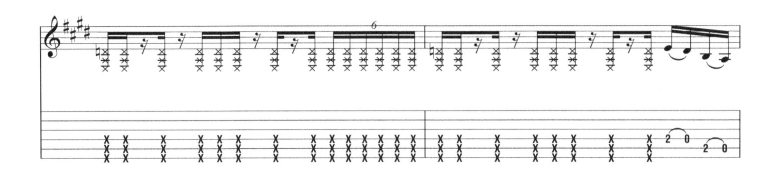

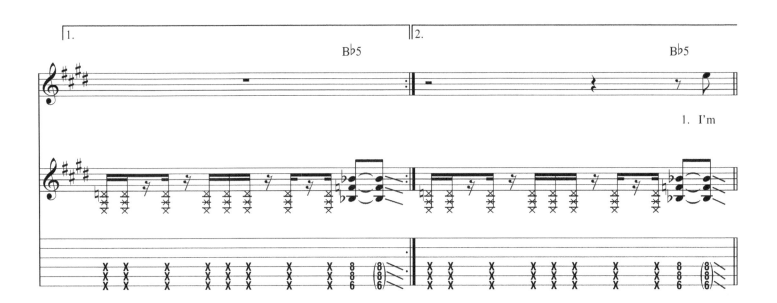

doing you a fa-vor, as I'm tak-ing all __ your mon-ey. I
2. See additional lyrics

guess I should __ feel sor-ry, but I don't e-ven trust __ me. There's some

bad news creep-ing up, ___ and you feel a sud-den chill. __ How do you do? __

___ My name is trou-ble, ___ I'm com-ing in __ for the kill. __

Pre-Chorus

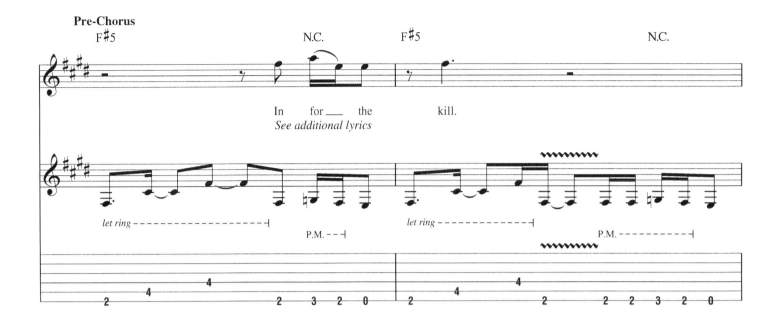

In for the kill.
See additional lyrics

Ooh, and you know I will, ooh.

Chorus

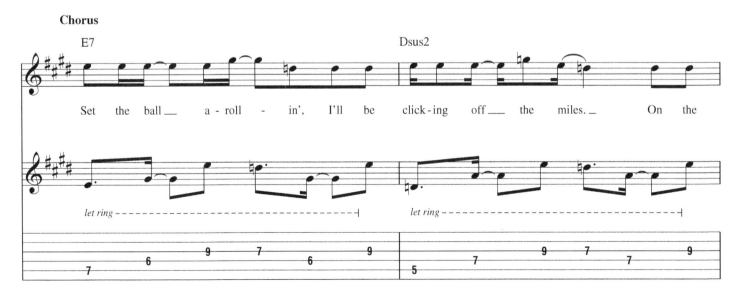

Set the ball a-roll-in', I'll be click-ing off the miles. On the

*Notes to right of slashes played by bass.

Interlude

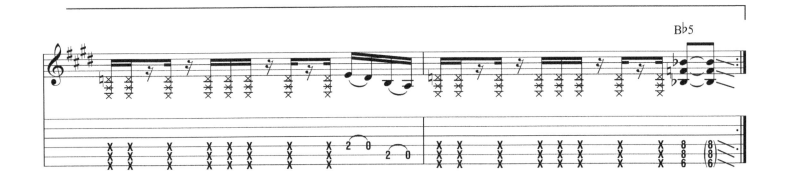

Bb5

2.

(C/E)   (A/F#)   **Interlude**
                                          N.C.

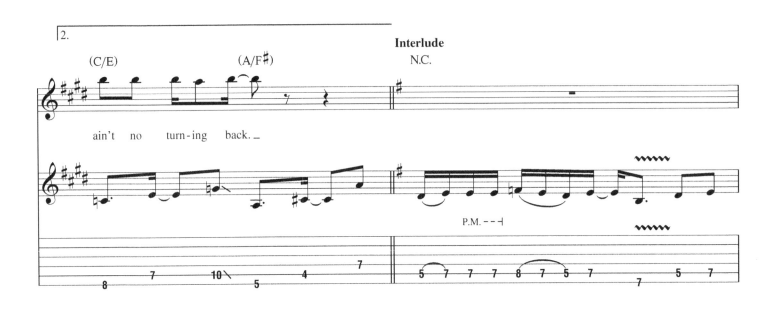

ain't   no   turn-ing   back. _

P.M. - - -|

                                    A5   E5   G5   A5

                          Guitar Solo
C   A5 N.C.(A)   N.C.

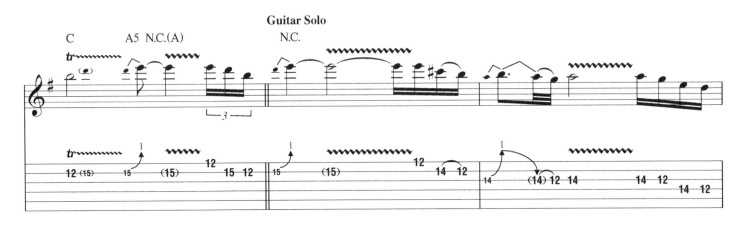

2nd time, substitute Fill 1

Set the ball __ a - roll - in', I'll be click-ing off __ the miles. __ On the

train of con - se-quenc - es, my box - car life o' style. __ My

think-ing is __ de - railed, _____ I'm tied __ up to the tracks. __ The

Additional Lyrics

2. No horse ever ran as fast as the money that you bet.
   I'm blowing on my cards, and I play them to my chest.
   Life's fabric is corrupt, shot through with corroded thread.
   As for me, I hocked my brains, packed my bags and headed west, ah.

Pre-Chorus I hocked my brains,
   Headed west, oh.

GUITAR NOTATION LEGEND

THE MUSICAL STAFF shows pitches and rhythms and is divided by bar lines into measures. Pitches are named after the first seven letters of the alphabet.

TABLATURE graphically represents the guitar fingerboard. Each horizontal line represents a string, and each number represents a fret.

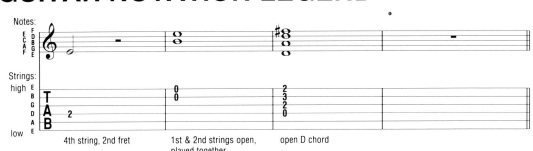

4th string, 2nd fret | 1st & 2nd strings open, played together | open D chord

HALF-STEP BEND: Strike the note and bend up 1/2 step.

WHOLE-STEP BEND: Strike the note and bend up one step.

GRACE NOTE BEND: Strike the note and immediately bend up as indicated.

SLIGHT (MICROTONE) BEND: Strike the note and bend up 1/4 step.

BEND AND RELEASE: Strike the note and bend up as indicated, then release back to the original note. Only the first note is struck.

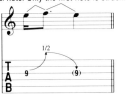

PRE-BEND: Bend the note as indicated, then strike it.

VIBRATO: The string is vibrated by rapidly bending and releasing the note with the fretting hand.

PALM MUTING: The note is partially muted by the pick hand lightly touching the string(s) just before the bridge.

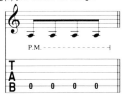

HAMMER-ON: Strike the first (lower) note with one finger, then sound the higher note (on the same string) with another finger by fretting it without picking.

PULL-OFF: Place both fingers on the notes to be sounded. Strike the first note and without picking, pull the finger off to sound the second (lower) note.

LEGATO SLIDE: Strike the first note and then slide the same fret-hand finger up or down to the second note. The second note is not struck.

SHIFT SLIDE: Same as legato slide, except the second note is struck.

TRILL: Very rapidly alternate between the notes indicated by continuously hammering on and pulling off.

TAPPING: Hammer ("tap") the fret indicated with the pick-hand index or middle finger and pull off to the note fretted by the fret hand.

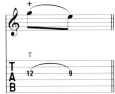

NATURAL HARMONIC: Strike the note while the fret-hand lightly touches the string directly over the fret indicated.

PINCH HARMONIC: The note is fretted normally and a harmonic is produced by adding the edge of the thumb or the tip of the index finger of the pick hand to the normal pick attack.

TREMOLO PICKING: The note is picked as rapidly and continuously as possible.

VIBRATO BAR DIVE AND RETURN: The pitch of the note or chord is dropped a specified number of steps (in rhythm), then returned to the original pitch.

VIBRATO BAR SCOOP: Depress the bar just before striking the note, then quickly release the bar.

VIBRATO BAR DIP: Strike the note and then immediately drop a specified number of steps, then release back to the original pitch.

Additional Musical Definitions

(accent)

- Accentuate note (play it louder).

(staccato)

- Play the note short.

D.S. al Coda

- Go back to the sign (%), then play until the measure marked "***To Coda***," then skip to the section labelled "**Coda**."

D.C. al Fine

- Go back to the beginning of the song and play until the measure marked "***Fine***" (end).

Fill

- Label used to identify a brief melodic figure which is to be inserted into the arrangement.

N.C.

- Harmony is implied.

- Repeat measures between signs.

- When a repeated section has different endings, play the first ending only the first time and the second ending only the second time.

Hal•Leonard® GUITAR PLAY-ALONG

AUDIO ACCESS INCLUDED

INCLUDES TAB

This series will help you play your favorite songs quickly and easily. Just follow the tab and listen to the CD or online audio to hear how the guitar should sound, and then play along using the separate backing tracks. Playback tools are provided for slowing down the tempo without changing pitch and looping challenging parts. The melody and lyrics are included in the book so that you can sing or simply follow along.

1. ROCK
00699570.................................$16.99

2. ACOUSTIC
00699569.................................$16.99

3. HARD ROCK
00699573.................................$17.99

4. POP/ROCK
00699571.................................$16.99

6. '90S ROCK
00699572.................................$16.99

7. BLUES
00699575.................................$17.99

8. ROCK
00699585.................................$16.99

9. EASY ACOUSTIC SONGS
00151708.................................$16.99

10. ACOUSTIC
00699586.................................$16.95

11. EARLY ROCK
0699579...................................$14.95

12. POP/ROCK
00699587.................................$14.95

13. FOLK ROCK
00699581.................................$16.99

14. BLUES ROCK
00699582.................................$16.99

15. R&B
00699583.................................$16.99

16. JAZZ
00699584.................................$15.95

17. COUNTRY
00699588.................................$16.99

18. ACOUSTIC ROCK
00699577.................................$15.95

19. SOUL
00699578.................................$15.99

20. ROCKABILLY
00699580.................................$16.99

21. SANTANA
00174525.................................$17.99

22. CHRISTMAS
00699600.................................$15.99

23. SURF
00699635.................................$15.99

24. ERIC CLAPTON
00699649.................................$17.99

25. THE BEATLES
00198265.................................$17.99

26. ELVIS PRESLEY
00699643.................................$16.99

27. DAVID LEE ROTH
00699645.................................$16.95

28. GREG KOCH
00699646.................................$16.99

29. BOB SEGER
00699647.................................$15.99

30. KISS
00699644.................................$16.99

31. CHRISTMAS HITS
00699652.................................$14.95

32. THE OFFSPRING
00699653.................................$14.95

33. ACOUSTIC CLASSICS
00699656.................................$17.99

34. CLASSIC ROCK
00699658.................................$17.99

35. HAIR METAL
00699660.................................$17.99

36. SOUTHERN ROCK
00699661.................................$16.95

37. ACOUSTIC METAL
00699662.................................$22.99

38. BLUES
00699663.................................$16.95

39. '80S METAL
00699664.................................$16.99

40. INCUBUS
00699668.................................$17.95

41. ERIC CLAPTON
00699669.................................$17.99

42. COVER BAND HITS
00211597.................................$16.99

43. LYNYRD SKYNYRD
00699681.................................$17.95

44. JAZZ
00699689.................................$16.99

45. TV THEMES
00699718.................................$14.95

46. MAINSTREAM ROCK
00699722.................................$16.95

47. HENDRIX SMASH HITS
00699723.................................$19.99

48. AEROSMITH CLASSICS
00699724.................................$17.99

49. STEVIE RAY VAUGHAN
00699725.................................$17.99

50. VAN HALEN 1978-1984
00110269.................................$17.99

51. ALTERNATIVE '90S
00699727.................................$14.99

52. FUNK
00699728.................................$15.99

53. DISCO
00699729.................................$14.99

54. HEAVY METAL
00699730.................................$15.99

55. POP METAL
00699731.................................$14.95

56. FOO FIGHTERS
00699749.................................$15.99

58. BLINK-182
00699772.................................$14.95

59. CHET ATKINS
00702347.................................$16.99

60. 3 DOORS DOWN
00699774.................................$14.95

61. SLIPKNOT
00699775.................................$16.99

62. CHRISTMAS CAROLS
00699798.................................$12.95

63. CREEDENCE CLEARWATER REVIVAL
00699802.................................$16.99

64. OZZY OSBOURNE
00699803.................................$17.99

66. THE ROLLING STONES
00699807.................................$17.99

67. BLACK SABBATH
00699808.................................$16.99

68. PINK FLOYD – DARK SIDE OF THE MOON
00699809.................................$16.99

69. ACOUSTIC FAVORITES
00699810.................................$16.99

70. OZZY OSBOURNE
00699805.................................$16.99

71. CHRISTIAN ROCK
00699824.................................$14.95

72. ACOUSTIC '90S
00699827.................................$14.95

73. BLUESY ROCK
00699829.................................$16.99

74. SIMPLE STRUMMING SONGS
00151706.................................$19.99

75. TOM PETTY
00699882.................................$16.99

76. COUNTRY HITS
00699884.................................$14.95

77. BLUEGRASS
00699910.................................$15.99

78. NIRVANA
00700132.................................$16.99

79. NEIL YOUNG
00700133.................................$24.99

80. ACOUSTIC ANTHOLOGY
00700175.................................$19.95

81. ROCK ANTHOLOGY
00700176.................................$22.99

82. EASY ROCK SONGS
00700177.................................$14.99

83. THREE CHORD SONGS
00700178.................................$16.99

84. STEELY DAN
00700200.................................$16.99

0418